6.50

Storrs Lectures on Jurisprudence
Yale Law School, 1979

The Decline of
the Rehabilitative Ideal

PENAL POLICY AND SOCIAL PURPOSE

Francis A. Allen

New Haven and London
Yale University Press

Designed by Nancy Ovedovitz
and set in Baskerville type.
Printed in the United States of America by
The Murray Printing Co., Westford, Mass.

Library of Congress Cataloging in Publication Data

Allen, Francis A
    The decline of the rehabilitative ideal.

    (Storrs lectures on jurisprudence; 1979)
    Includes bibliographical references and index.
    1.   Rehabilitation of criminals—United States.
2.   Corrections—United States.   I.   Title.
II.   Series.
HV9304.A62   365'.66   80-25098
ISBN 0–300–02565–3

10   9   8   7   6   5   4   3   2   1

TO MARK WALSH ALLEN

My warmhearted, stouthearted friend
and grandson

"Neither is it possible to discover the more remote and deeper parts of any science, if you stand but upon the level of the same science."

Francis Bacon

CONTENTS

PREFACE

This book addresses themes with which I have been concerned for a quarter of a century. What I have called the rehabilitative ideal is important as an issue for penology, but it may be even more interesting and significant when seen as a problem for broader policy analysis and social inquiry. In any event, this is what I have attempted in the pages that follow.

Even a small volume permits a fuller and more rounded discussion of its themes than was possible in an oral presentation as the William L. Storrs Lectures at Yale Law School on October 8–10, 1979. Dean Harry Wellington and the Law School faculty greeted Mrs. Allen and me with a kindness and hospitality that made our stay in New Haven in every way pleasant and memorable. I also wish to thank Dean Wellington for his unperturbed patience during delays of several years when the lectures were being prepared. His unreasonable confidence that the job would get done contributed to its completion. Thanks should also be given to the John Simon Guggenheim Memorial Foundation for the award of a fellowship during 1978. I am especially grateful to the foundation for supporting my work a second time. The William W. Cook Fund of the University of Michigan Law School also again came to my assistance. My thanks are strongly felt.

Giving adequate acknowledgments to intellectual contributions is a harder task. Of the many who deserve thanks, I shall mention four young legal scholars. Robert A. Burt, now of Yale Law School, bears the heavy responsibility for inducing me to return, after many years, to the theme of penal rehabilitation. Employing the high lawyer's skills of persuasion and benign duress, he argued that I was under a professional and perhaps moral obligation to look again at the rehabilitative ideal in the modern context. I did not entirely understand Mr. Burt's argument but was, nevertheless, persuaded by it. Frank Zimring of the University of Chicago Law School faculty lavished his remarkable creativity and enthusiasm on my project from the beginning. Echoes of his insights are to be heard throughout the book. My colleague Richard O. Lempert read the manuscript and in his typically pentrating way improved it both in form and in substance. Carl E. Schneider, who will shortly begin his career as a law teacher at the University of Michigan, served as my student research assistant and prepared a memorandum on the antebellum penitentiary movement of such distinction that it has since been published under his own name. I have made frequent use of his paper in the following pages. These four young men are entitled to have it said that they are responsible for none of the book's deficiencies; but anyone familiar with their work would know that anyway.

Like any other book, the preparation of this one entailed a large amount of secretarial drudgery. Denise Bonsall met these demands with a tolerance and good humor that I greatly appreciate.

My wife, June, made contributions without number to the writing of this book, as to everything I do. She is unaware of many of them, which is itself a gift.

O N E

The Rehabilitative Ideal and the Decline of Social Purpose

The most striking characteristic of modern legal thought is its concern with questions of public policy. In other times, such an interest, while never absent from the law, was neither so dominant nor so undisguised as in the recent past. For better or worse, the erecting of elegant structures of judicial precedent and demonstrations of the historical authenticity of legal doctrine have become, for the present, objectives of less importance.[1] Recently it has been argued that some earlier periods of American legal history displayed concern for the wider social impact of the law comparable in intensity to that of the present. However this may be, one can hardly overlook this tendency in the half-century just past.

No attempt will be made in these pages to construct a general theory of policy analysis. It is worth noting, however, that the decline of what I have called the rehabilitative ideal provides a prime opportunity for considering the relations of law and opinion, for observing the impact of changes in cultural and political attitudes on penal policy. The opportunity is prime, because the phenomena under consideration involve a set of ideas, goals, and institutional practices that had their first flowering in antebellum America and later dominated penological thought throughout most of the twentieth century. In the course of a decade, perhaps less, the rehabilitative ideal suffered a precipitous decline in its capacity to influence American penal practice and, more important, in its potency to define commonly held aspirations in the penal area.

Other motives may underlie a study of these events. Certainly they are of high importance for those professionally concerned with the formulation and application of American penal policy. The decline of the rehabilitative ideal suggests that one active in this field may now be confronted with a set of social limitations that severely constrict both the objectives that he may prudently pursue and the means available to achieve them. The study may be justified in quite different ways, however. One may be drawn to these phenomena, not because of professional concerns with penological administration, but because one suspects that the decline of the rehabilitative ideal has something of interest to say about the society in which the system of justice functions. Many years ago the late Mr. Justice Oliver Wendell Holmes remarked: "The law is a small subject (though . . . it leads to all things)."[2] Here as elsewhere, a study of movements in legal policy may provide an avenue to understanding the larger world of which the law and its institutions are a part.[3]

The rehabilitative ideal concept requires description and amplification. It is not surprising to discover that the phrase embraces great complexity and, indeed, encompasses widely different and even conflicting kinds of social policies. One may begin by saying that the rehabilitative ideal is the notion that a primary purpose of penal treatment is to effect changes in the characters, attitudes, and behavior of convicted offenders, so as to strengthen the social defense against unwanted behavior, but also to contribute to the welfare and satisfactions of offenders.[4] Having so said, however, one has hardly done more than express, perhaps imperfectly, a least common denominator of the myriad expressions of the rehabilitative ideal that have contended for recognition in the twentieth century and in earlier history. It is not profitable to attempt a taxonomy of all versions of the rehabilitative ideal, but some sense of the possible variations will advance the discussion that follows.

It is well to identify some of the questions left untouched by broad description of the rehabilitative ideal. The description does not specify a theory about crime causation; and in fact, theories of rehabilitation have been advanced by those who view crime as a product of moral default of offenders, by persons who assume the social causation of crime, and even by some who attribute it to individual biological propensities.[5] The definition, in other words, does not resolve the perennial controversies between freedom of the will and determinism, although modern expressions of the rehabilitative ideal lean heavily to the latter.

Again, the nature of the rehabilitative ideal is profoundly affected by whether rehabilitation is seen as the *exclusive* justification of penal sanctions (as was very nearly the stance of some exuberant American theorists in mid-twentieth century), as a dominant purpose, or only as a part of a penal strategy that may sometimes require rehabilitative objectives to give way to other important social interests. Clearly, too, the content of the rehabilitative ideal is significantly affected by the means employed and assumed to be effective in achieving rehabilitation. A remarkable range of rehabilitative techniques has been espoused in the United States, including the use of the treadmill and the cat-o'-nine-tails.[6] The position of the great eighteenth-century English prison-reformer, John Howard, provides a convenient benchmark for these comparisons. Howard's motivations were formidably humanitarian. For him rehabilitative technique consisted of moral and religious exhortation, order, and providing adequate drains in the jails.[7] Obviously, the meanings and impact of the rehabilitative ideal are quite different depending on whether the appropriate means are thought to be the promotion of literacy, the provision of vocational education, programs of psychotherapy, brainwashing, or the surgical removal of brain tissue. Of central importance are the larger purposes of the rehabilitative effort, whether to preserve traditional political and moral values or to hasten arrival of the brave new world.

The roots of the rehabilitative ideal lie deep in Western society. In the Old Testament emphasis on the correctional potential of punishment is explicit. Punishment is recommended as an essential feature of child rearing. The wise father will chasten his son "betimes."[8] The analogy of the loving father, moreover, is used to explain the ways of God to man. The rod of Yahweh is wielded to purify the sons of Levi.[9] Some of these ideas were part of the common coin of Greek civilization, so much a part of folk wisdom, in fact, that they became fair game for the satire of Aristophanes. In *The Clouds* a son undertakes to justify the beating of his tottering old father: a father, he argues, chastises a son because he loves and cherishes him; and when the father enters second childhood he must likewise be "taught" by the loving blows of his son.[10] More to the point, the Greeks perceived correction as a legitimate part of state policy. In Aristotle punishment is seen "as a kind of cure."[11] In the *Laws*, Plato sketches the outline of a penal program remarkably modern in purpose and form.[12]

This strand of thought continues in the writings of the medieval churchmen. Augustine supports legitimate punishment "such as society permits" as a means of improvement of the offender and so that he may "be readjusted to family harmony from which he dislodged himself."[13] Thomas Aquinas concurs with the observation that "fraternal correction is an act of charity."[14] The rehabilitative ideal also found articulation in the early modern period, in the eighteenth-century Enlightenment, and in the century that followed.[15]

There are two important reasons for noting the persistence of the rehabilitative ideal across time and its emergence in widely differing cultures. First, even brief reference to this history demonstrates that the meanings and tendencies of the rehabilitative ideal can be grasped only when considered in relation to the particular cultural contexts in which it arises. Twentieth-century expressions of the rehabilitative ideal, for example, may be seen as part of a modern faith in therapeutic interventions, often with purposes extending far beyond penological treatment and encompassing the health and happiness of society generally. The astonishing agenda of the mental hygiene movement in the years immediately following the Second World War are illustrative. Industrial productivity, domestic tranquillity, and international peace are only a few of the objectives that have been confidently projected.[16] Any attempt to understand the rehabilitative ideal in the modern administration of criminal justice apart from this background is likely to prove unproductive. There is a second observation, however. The history of the rehabilitative ideal far antedates modern therapeutics. This fact may prove relevant in the future consideration of possible alternative forms of rehabilitative effort.

Appreciation of the decline of the rehabilitative ideal in the 1970s requires an accurate understanding of its dominance in the United States for most of the twentieth century. In *Williams* v. *New York*, Mr. Justice Black, speaking for the Supreme Court of the United States in 1949, referred to "a prevalent modern philosophy of penology that the punishment should fit the offender and not merely the crime." "Retribution," he added, "is no longer the dominant objective of the criminal law. Reformation and rehabilitation of offenders have become important goals of criminal jurisprudence."[17] There can be no doubt that Justice Black's dictum expressed the enlightened opinion, not only of the judiciary, but also of the public at large. A characteristic irony in the *Williams* case should be noted in passing. In its opinion the Court upheld the use of a typical instrument of modern rehabilitationism, a pre-sentence report. The report contained statements of a probation officer highly prejudicial to the convicted offender, statements that apparently induced the trial judge to disregard the jury's recommendation of mercy and to impose a sentence of death on the defendant. Here as in many other modern instances, incapacitation can be seen competing with and often prevailing over mitigation in the practical administration of the rehabilitative ideal.

Perhaps the most tangible evidences of the dominance of the rehabilitative ideal are found in its legislative expressions. Almost all of the characteristic innovations in criminal justice in this century are reflections of the rehabilitative ideal: the juvenile court, the indeterminate sentence, systems of probation and parole, the youth authority, and the promise (if not the reality) of therapeutic programs in prisons, juvenile institutions, and mental hospitals. Frequently, of course, the projected objectives were not achieved; and the tendency of the rehabilitative ideal to become debased and to serve unarticulated social purposes will require further consideration. Nevertheless, it is remarkable how widely the rehabilitative ideal was accepted in this century as a statement of aspirations for the penal system, a statement largely endorsed by the media, politicians, and ordinary citizens.

It was in the universities, however, that the dominance of the rehabilitative ideal became most firmly established. Significant university concern with criminological research and theory in the United States dates from the years immediately preceding the First World War, and the subsequent development of these interests was associated with the rise of the sciences of human behavior on American campuses in the first half of this century. Academic criminology, of course, did not confine its attention to the theories and practices of penal treatment. A large and conflicting literature on crime causation emerged, displaying etiological theories variously emphasizing social structure and ecology, learning theory, psychic disturbance, cultural constraint, and biological determinism. Yet even a brief glance at the college criminology textbooks in wide use at midcentury clearly reveals the importance accorded penological treatment in criminological thought and the almost unchallenged sway of the rehabilitative ideal.[18] The emergence of social work and the "helping professions" strongly reinforced these tendencies. Because academic interests were so largely engaged in therapeutic strategy, much university research accepted the convicted offender as a given. Questions of crime definition and guilt determination were ignored or neglected until the cultural explosions of the late 1960s upset prevailing assumptions and defined new concerns.[19] Research into such fundamental problems as the deterrent efficacy of penal sanctions was avoided and even scorned. This history strikingly illustrates how an ideology ensconced in an academic discipline may dictate what questions are to be investigated.[20] In the larger community periodic agitations about the American "crime problem" produced temporary defections from the rehabilitative ideal. The universities, however, provided bastions of defense, a support not seriously eroded until the decade of the 1970s.

At the beginning of that decade an influential report on penal justice issued by the American Friends Service Committee could still say: "Despite [its] shortcomings the treatment approach receives nearly unanimous support from those working in the field of criminal justice, even the most progressive and humanitarian."[21] Such a statement could not have been made in the mid-1970s. Indeed, the report itself, with its fervent attack on the rehabilitative ideal by a group historically associated with its emergence and flowering in the United States, signaled the wide and precipitious decline of penal rehabilitationism that was to characterize the years ahead.

Again it is the legislative manifestations that provide the most tangible evidences of the new tendencies. The California sentencing act of 1976 serves as a useful indicator. The 1976 act repealed older sentencing provisions whose over-riding purposes, according to a California court, were to "maximize rehabilitary efforts."[22] The new law states in accents not heard a decade earlier: "The Legislature finds and declares that the purpose of imprisonment for crime is punishment. This purpose is best served by terms proportionate to the seriousness of the offense with provision for uniformity in the sentences of offenders committing the same offense under similar circumstances."[23] The California law is representative of a spate of legislative proposals, enacted or advocated throughout the country, that attack the statutory expressions of the rehabilitative ideal. The objects of this attack are sentencing discretion, the indeterminate sentence, the parole function, the uses of probation in cases of serious criminality, and even allowances of "good time" credit in the prisons.[24] Some of the new legislation seeks to impose the assumptions of adult criminality on the operations of the juvenile court.[25] The spectacle of three dozen American states scrambling to enact valid death-penalty legislation in recent years may in part reflect similar tendencies.[26]

The new laws are not necessarily the most significant indications of what has occurred. The same may be said of the efforts to summon the public to a new crusade against crime and criminals that have filled the channels of communications during the last decade. American attitudes toward crime and its control since the early nineteenth century have been typically amnesic—there have been periods of surprise and angry agitation about the prevalence of crime followed by intervals of somnolence and unconcern.[27] The present fretful attention being given to the American crime problem has perhaps persisted longer and reached higher levels of intensity than some comparable periods in the past; it is, nevertheless, part of a recognizable historical pattern. What is most significant about the 1970s, and what distinguishes it from the past, is the degree to which the rehabilitative ideal has suffered defections, not only from politicians, editorial writers, and the larger public, but also from scholars and professionals in criminology, penology, and the law.

The erosion of intellectual support for the rehabilitative ideal, both in and out of the universities, resulted in a profusion of ideological positions. One of these currents of thought antedated the 1970s, having become prominent during the excitements of Vietnam and racial militancy in the late 1960s. A school of radical criminology arose that identified criminal justice with the interest of the stronger. Rehabilitative efforts were seen as merely part of the mechanisms of social control, as machinery devised and operated to oppress the poor and powerless and to advance the economic and political interests of the dominant social classes.[28] A second strain of thought avoided the revolutionary implications of radical criminology but nevertheless took positions at least equally hostile to the rehabilitative ideal. This view emphasized moral autonomy and expressed an egalitarian politics. Its concepts of just punishment conflicted with the deterministic tendencies of the rehabilitative ideal, and its political orientation was antagonistic to the disparities of treatment and the unregulated discretion associated with modern rehabilitationism.[29] Still another current of thought in the universities tended to give strong emphasis to the value of public order. It generally favored an escalation of enforcement powers and efforts and expressed an unequivocal skepticism about the rehabilitative capacities of the state.[30] This program and the assumptions underlying it were carried to extreme application by a fourth group— those whose purposes were almost entirely repressive, whose views of crime and its control might be described as the "war theory" of criminal justice.[31]

These positions were founded on differing assumptions and motivated by widely diverging purposes. Because they possessed the common characteristic of opposition to rehabilitative theories of penal treatment, however, adherents of these various and often conflicting views sometimes united in support of particular proposals for legislative and institutional reform. In the areas of penal policy, the 1970s was an era of strange bedfellows.

Although judgments may vary about precisely how far support for rehabilitative theories of penal treatment has eroded, and estimates differ about their likely revival in the future, the central fact appears inescapable: the rehabilitative ideal has declined in the United States; the decline has been substantial, and it has been precipitous. When one moves from the phenomenon itself to inquiries about its causes, however, the footing becomes less secure. Nevertheless, certain judgments can prudently be asserted. One of these is that the decline of the rehabilitative ideal in the 1970s cannot be explained satisfactorily as the consequence of the rational cases arrayed against it. Indeed, the profusion of ideological positions that arose in opposition to rehabilitative theories is part of the phenomenon to be explained. The very diversity of the attacks on the rehabilitative ideal, their conflicting assumptions and motivations, and the suddenness of the decline suggest that broader social and cultural influences are involved.

Although the literature protesting the hegemony of the rehabilitative ideal cannot be accepted as a sufficient cause for its decline, portions of that literature may assist efforts at broader understanding. One book in particular, Anthony Platt's *The Child Savers*, will be mentioned.[32] This work constitutes a vigorous attack on the juvenile court and the movement that has supported it. The author's thesis is that the juvenile court was created as an instrument to impose the values of the dominant nineteenth-century bourgeoisie on the children of immigrants crowding into American cities. The subsequent history of the court is likewise characterized by the coercive infliction of middle-class values on the poor, the oppressed, and racial minorities. It is no part of my purpose to appraise or challenge this thesis. Yet the argument suggests interesting questions. The first is this: What characteristics would likely be revealed by any society in which a vigorous rehabilitative ideal emerges and flourishes? And again: Is it not likely that a thriving rehabilitative ideal presupposes a society in which the dominant groups possess high confidence in their definitions of character and their standards of good behavior, in which resort to the public force to advance and defend those values is seen not only as appropriate but as very nearly inevitable?

A clear statement of the cultural conditions favorable to the emergence and survival of rehabilitative theory would surely advance analysis of the recent decline of the rehabilitative ideal in the United States. In the discussion that follows, an effort, however incomplete, will be made to state such a thesis and to illustrate and test it. The first of the analytic propositions to be tested is that the rehabilitative ideal is likely to arise and persist in societies in which there is strong and widespread belief in the malleability of human character and behavior. There is, of course, a large element of tautology in this statement, for rehabilitation is by definition a character-changing and behavior-changing procedure, and its underlying assumption cannot be entertained in a community that totally rejects these possibilities. There are, however, significant differences of degree in the optimism manifested toward such possibilities among different cultures and in the same society over time. Moreover, the question may be less a matter of abstract faith in the malleability of human beings than of the degree of confidence a society can muster in the capacities of its institutions to effect desirable guidance to character development and alterations in troublesome behavior. The second proposition is that a flourishing rehabilitative ideal requires a sufficient consensus of values to make possible a working agreement on what it means to be rehabilitated, on the distinction between the malady and the cure.

According to the thesis advanced, then, these are the cultural presuppositions of a flourishing rehabilitative ideal: a vibrant faith in the malleability of human beings and a workable consensus on the goals of treatment. In the discussion that follows the procedure will be to examine—necessarily perfunctorily—two widely different societies in which the rehabilitative ideal emerged and thrived to determine whether in them the suggested conditions were satisfied. Following this, the same questions will be put to American society in the 1970s.

There is historical warrant for the assertion that some of the first important institutional expressions of the rehabilitative ideal in the Western world emerged in nineteenth-century antebellum America.[33] Some writers, no doubt, have overstated the distinctively American aspects of the penitentiary movement in the United States, for these developments had strong antecedents in the traditions of European religious and humanitarian thought and in the intellectual currents of the Enlightenment.[34] Yet that the American experiments contained much that was important is attested by the procession of foreign prison visitors drawn to these shores, including two young French intellectuals, Gustave de Beaumont and Alexis de Tocqueville, who arrived in 1831 to prepare a report on the penitentiary system in the United States.[35]

The rehabilitative ideal became an important element in practical penological thought only when imprisonment became a principal mode of punishment.[36] The rise of the prison, in turn, was in significant part a product of the industrial revolution. It is not literally true that imprisonment for punishment, as contrasted to detention pending trial or the infliction of other punishments, was unheard of in earlier times.[37] Yet a system of long-term incarceration is an economic indulgence, and one beyond the means of most Western societies until near the end of the eighteenth century. In the early nineteenth century the rise of imprisonment and the decline of alternative punishments posed serious questions about the practices and purposes of imprisonment. The answer given in Pennsylvania and later in New York was that penal practice must be directed to rehabilitative ends. The means employed appear today harsh and bizarre, and the excitement and discipleship they produced, not only in other American states but also in much of Western Europe, can hardly be credited today. The Pennsylvania procedures contemplated a regime of solitary confinement interrupted by occasional interludes of religious exhortation.[38] In New York, largely because of fiscal considerations, a different tack was taken. At Auburn Prison the famous "silent system" was introduced in which prisoners worked and ate together but in strict silence.[39] Both systems attempted to avoid the moral contagions thought to result when inmates communicate among themselves and placed strong reliance on regimentation and harsh discipline to inculcate habits of industry and good behavior. Each regime, at least in its beginnings, assumed the malleability of its inmates; and these pioneering efforts at rehabilitation were viewed with pride by many Americans. "That community which first conceived the idea of abandoning the principle of mere physical force even in respect to prisons, and of treating their inmates as redeemable beings," wrote one contemporary, " . . . must occupy an elevated place in the scale of political or social civilization."[40]

Similar optimism about the malleability of human character was revealed in other rehabilitative strategies. Preventive programs, particularly those directed to juveniles, received significant support, as is illustrated by the establishment of "houses of refuge" in several American cities during the 1820s.[41] Persons who become delinquent, noted Beaumont and Tocqueville, "have been unfortunate before they became guilty."[42] This and similar observations expose concerns of the time with other aspects of human malleability—those relating to the causes of crime. Questions of criminal responsibility became a staple theme of the popular literature, and many writers implicated social institutions as a principal cause of crime.[43] "The evil is in the collective action of the race," wrote Arthur Brisbane.[44] The Boston clergyman, Theodore Parker, inquired, "How can it be justice to punish as a crime that which the institutions of society render unavoidable?"[45] If society produces criminals, then society must undo its mischief through programs of prevention and rehabilitation.

The movements in the theory and practices of criminal justice occurred in a society substantially committed to the perfectibility of human beings and the improvement of social institutions. The antebellum period in the United States, at least in the North, was the great age of reform.[46] In an essay significantly entitled "Man the Reformer," Ralph Waldo Emerson remarked in 1841: "In the history of the world the doctrine of reform had never such scope as at the present hour. . . . Not a kingdom, town, statute, rite, calling, man, or woman, but is threatened by the new spirit."[47] It was in this era that the American faith in public education as the indispensable precondition of a flourishing republican society gained wide concurrence.[48] Religious evangelism, departing from earlier emphases, mandated self-improvement and the amelioration of social conditions.[49] These common tendencies were reflected even in economic enterprise. The values expressed in economic activity were those of initiative, change, and reconstruction, not the quiet enjoyment of vested property interests. The initiatives of the business community matched the ideological entrepreneurship of the reformers.[50] Indeed, in many cases the individuals were the same.

A society as individualistic and pluralistic as antebellum America might be expected to display a diversity rather than a consensus of values in many important areas. Such conflicts and diversities did in fact exist. The sharp differences in assumptions and attitudes between North and South, for example, are frequently noted by Tocqueville; and the widening schism of values concerning human slavery hung over most of the period like a pall.[51] But the consensus of values relevant to a flourishing rehabilitative ideal relates to the goals of rehabilitative effort, and in this area a workable accord was reached. This is best seen in the enthusiastic regard held for the family as the source of character and right conduct. Some historians have detected a surge of domesticity in the nineteenth century.[52] In a little known case none other than John Marshall is found asserting that the "harmony of society" is dependent on the "mutual partiality" and the "delicate forebearance" of husband and wife.[53] Not only were the values cultivated in a virtuous family those that were considered to be the goals of rehabilitation, but the family was taken as the model for rehabilitative treatment in the cases in which the natural family could not or would not perform its functions.[54] This tradition extends into the twentieth century. The first juvenile court law, enacted in 1899, and widely copied thereafter, directs that the treatment accorded wards of the court shall resemble "as nearly as may be" that provided children by wise parents.[55]

The tendencies of the antebellum period just described did not of course go unchallenged. The period abounds in countertendencies, dissonance, and uncertainties. Underlying the intellectual ferment and the social and political activism were certain imperfectly resolved conflicts. Very different postures were taken toward the future. For some it was to be eagerly awaited as an era of unlimited possibilities freed from the illiberal contraints of the past. Others feared the future of a society in which the old categories were dissolving and in which the prospect might well be anarchy in morals and politics.[56] One needs only to recall the names of Hawthorne and Melville to demonstrate that a vibrant optimism about the perfectibility of human beings is an incomplete description of antebellum tendencies.[57] Even in the areas of criminal justice skepticism about the rehabilitative potential of the new penitentiaries was frequently expressed, and among some actually involved in administration of the systems, hopes for inmate reform were almost wholly rejected.[58] Indeed, most of the counts in the modern indictment of the rehabilitative ideal were expressed by one person or another before the outbreak of the American Civil War. These countertendencies and ambivalences demonstrate that antebellum America, like other historical periods, cannot be captured fully within the confines of a formula. The blurring of the pattern, however, does not diminish the reality of the tendencies noticed earlier; for a robust faith in the possibilities of individual and social improvement was expressed in antebellum America and a workable consensus of values proved possible. It seems responsible to conclude, therefore, that the hypothesized conditions of a flourishing rehabilitative ideal were satisfied in the American society of that time.

Among advanced societies few contrasts are more extreme than those between antebellum America and the People's Republic of China. Yet a version of the rehabilitative ideal flourishes in the modern Chinese penal system. Rehabilitationism in China emerged in a society that expresses perhaps the strongest faith in the malleability of human beings of any in the modern world. Attitudes toward malleability, of course, reflect underlying theories of human nature; and the officially propagated theories of the People's Republic emphatically reject the existence of innate human attributes that seriously limit the possibilities of change in human thought and action.[59] Chinese policy reflects an optimism about the acceleration of change through the use of social measures operating directly on the thoughts and attitudes of the people, and in doing so moves beyond traditional Marxist views associating behavioral and character change with alterations in class structure and property relations.[60] In such a society education is likely to be viewed as a powerful collective resource available to advance community purposes, and such is true of modern China.[61]

In large measure, Chinese penal practice represents a special application of the theories of human nature that pervade that society.[62] Chinese legislation expressly avows the rehabilitative purposes of the penal program.[63] These purposes are reflected at the outset of the penal process in the great importance accorded confessions of guilt. Such admissions are required to be detailed and exhaustive, and typically, to implicate others who share, or are believed to share, the prisoner's culpability. Confession serves more than immediate law-enforcement ends; it is also intended to overcome the prisoner's strategies of resistance, which, if not defeated, are thought to make true reformation impossible.[64] Strong emphasis is placed on techniques of group therapy. The obligation to study imposed on all prisoners takes its most important form in group discussions in which prisoners are expected to recognize and analyze their own failings, accept group criticism, and point out the transgressions of fellow inmates.[65] One slow to make an acceptable confession or chronically deficient in his prison behavior may be subjected to an extreme form of group encounter known as the struggle. The culprit is surrounded by a large group of his fellow prisoners and is made to endure their insults, contempt, and threats of violence, sometimes for long periods.[66] The purpose of the procedure is not only to subject the individual to intense group discipline, but also to influence the feelings and behavior of all others participating in the ritual. Ultimately, however, primary reliance appears to be placed on compulsory labor; and the confidence expressed in the rehabilitative potential of demanding work and rigorous discipline recalls similar attitudes displayed in nineteenth-century America.[67] The Chinese system exhibits other features that have often been associated with the rehabilitative ideal elsewhere, such as extreme indeterminacy in sentencing practice and a diminished conception of the rights of accused persons in criminal procedures.[68] Whatever conflicts in ideology are proceeding under the surface of Chinese life, a consensus of values about the ends of rehabilitative treatment seems to have been established. Much teaching in China is based on exemplary models of conduct. Both in and out of the penal system the objective appears to be the production of a human type who has cast aside merely private ends and is fully devoted to social purposes.[69]

As in any complex society, countertendencies can be discerned in Chinese practice. Convictions about the malleability of human behavior and dedication to rehabilitative objectives in the penal system have not diverted the Chinese from widespread resort to capital punishment in cases of those who owe what are known as blood debts or have outraged public sensibilities by committing other extremely serious crimes.[70] Also striking is the persistence of the disabilities inflicted on those of "bad" social class or political background and even on the children of such persons.[71] Nevertheless, the main tendencies of modern Chinese life, like those in the very different society of antebellum America, satisfy the suggested cultural conditions of a flourishing rehabilitative ideal: a vibrant faith in the malleability of human beings and a workable consensus on the ends of treatment. In both societies the rehabilitative ideal emerged and thrived, and in each a confident sense of destiny and social purpose is displayed.

Such attributes are not descriptive of the United States in the 1970s. In contrast, modern America reveals a radical loss of confidence in its political and social institutions and a significant diminishment in its sense of public purpose. The phenomenon has been widely noted both in the popular and scholarly literature. The continuities of human experience are such that widespread changes in basic attitudes and morale do not occur abruptly and without antecedents. Yet although the malaise of the 1970s has origins dating from the turn of the century and perhaps before, the causal factors combined to produce a new sensibility in the post-Hiroshima, post-Vietnam, post-Watergate world. The decline of the rehabilitative ideal may be seen as one aspect of this modern sensibility. For the purposes at hand, attention needs to be directed to the modern consciousness primarily as it affects confidence in the malleability of human beings and the capacity to achieve a workable consensus relating to the ends of rehabilitation. In arriving at judgments on these matters, principal reliance will, of necessity, be placed on published social commentary. It is assumed that such literature bears some significant relation to the reality it purports to describe.

There is much evidence that the traditional American optimism about the malleability of human behavior has not wholly evaporated. Strategies of self-improvement that played so large a part in the lives of individuals in the last century may be thought to have their modern counterparts in the rise of sectarian religion and the flourishing of a popular psychologism. Yet nineteenth-century beliefs in the perfectability of human nature have been profoundly weakened by such events in the intellectual history of the West as the Freudian revolution. Moreover, contemporary expressions of confidence in human malleability are often accompanied by a pervasive pessimism about the effectiveness and integrity of social institutions. It can hardly be supposed that Americans in the past were wholly unaware of institutional malfunctions, but a durable commitment to the ends and aspirations symbolized by the institutions overcame disappointments with institutional failures.[72] Such tolerance dwindled in the America of the 1970s. It is not only the institutions of criminal justice that have suffered significant losses of confidence. All the institutions traditionally relied on for socializing the young and directing human behavior to the achievement of social purposes have likewise sustained massive losses of confidence and corresponding erosions of morale. Scrutiny of contemporary attitudes toward the family, the schools, and what may be inexactly described as therapy, reveals deep-seated skepticism about the capacity of traditional institutions to achieve beneficial direction to human behavior and aspirations.

The displacement and diminution of family authority in the modern world constitute one of the most thoroughly documented phenomena in Western society. A generation ago George Orwell, commenting on the political implications of this diminution, wrote, "A deep instinct warns . . . not to destroy the family which in the modern world is the sole refuge from the state, but all the while the forces of the machine age are slowly destroying the family."[73] Even those not fully sharing Orwell's fears are compelled to recognize the significant differences in attitudes toward the family that distinguish modern from early nineteenth-century American society. The primacy of the family in child rearing, and hence in the creation and preservation of societal values, was vigorously asserted and confidently defended in the antebellum United States.[74] Traditions that penetrate thought and feelings so deeply do not die easily. Thus in 1972 the Supreme Court of the United States wrote, "[The] primary role of the parents in the upbringing of their children is now established beyond debate as an enduring American tradition."[75] Traditions may persist, however, after fundamental alterations in the underlying reality have occurred. The reality of the modern American family is that its authority in the area of child rearing has been significantly displaced by the state, the schools, "experts," peer groups, and the market.

Despite the lucubrations of the Supreme Court, public policy in the twentieth century has generally promoted increasingly broad interventions of state power into areas of decision making formerly reserved for parental authority. The strategy of the melting pot provided purpose and justification for incursions into the families of immigrants under the aegis of the schools, the juvenile court, and child welfare agencies.[76] The rise of sciences of human behavior provided a rationale for such interventions by transforming child rearing into an area of community concern demanding the ministrations of practitioners trained in medicine, social work, and other behavioral disciplines.[77] Nor were the claims of expertise confined to the families of the poor and powerless. The existence of a science of child rearing became accepted by middle-class parents, who, in short order, became more dependent than the poor on the dicta of the experts.[78] In some instances the further displacement of family authority is an unintended consequence of policies directed to important and laudable ends. Some persons intensely committed to relegating family relations to an expanding code of rights fail to recognize that rights are creatures of the law, and law is an instrumentality of state power. The results of such reforms are sometimes benign and may enhance the quality of family living. But persistent resort to state authority under the rubric of "rights" produces a penumbra effect: diminution of the privacy and hegemony of the family, even in areas in which no abuse of its individual members has occurred.[79]

Not all the forces with which parental authority contends, however, have their origins in the exercise of state power; some reflect cultural and economic movement. The competition provided family values by children's peer groups has been widely observed and experienced. As some commentators have noted, what is often most striking about the attitudes of youth culture toward parental values is not hostility, but a conviction of irrelevancy.[80] The market contributes its share to the displacement of parental authority. Current controversies relating to the regulation of television advertising directed to children disclose a struggle between the values of at least some parents and those of the media and manufacturers. Ironically, it is the federal government that proposes to monitor and referee the struggle.[81]

The displacement of family authority is, in part, both a cause and effect of a new set of attitudes about the nature and purposes of the family, attitudes radically at odds with those professed in antebellum America. Contemporary literature portrays a movement in the perception of the family from a hierarchical structure characterized by mandatory mutual obligations to an arrangement of convenience designed to advance the personal satisfactions and self-fulfillment of its individual members.[82] It is apparent that the latter perception allocates to the family a different and lesser role as an instrumentality for behavioral guidance and the creation and preservation of basic societal values. Certainly modern literature contains few encomiums of the family for its performance of character-building and socializing functions. Rather, the literature typically concerns itself with pathology—family dissolution and violent abuse of child and spouse—or the devising of new social arrangements as substitutes for the traditional family.[83]

Prevailing attitudes toward the schools constitute an important part of the social context of the rehabilitative ideal. Since programs of penal rehabilitation are in significant part educative in nature, one may expect to discover a close correlation between the degrees of optimism being manifested toward penal reform and those toward public education generally. This correlation is clearly discernible in modern China as it was in early nineteenth-century America.[84] In the 1970s, a period distinguished for acerbic appraisals of American institutions, few have been subjected to such relentless and comprehensive criticism as that meted out to the schools. All of the traditional claims made for American public education are challenged by its critics. The picture drawn is one of waste and futility. The schools are failing in their basic educational mission, and indeed, mass education is "intrinsically incompatible" with educational quality; the schools, it is said, are the principal enemy of true learning.[85] Jeffersonian theory conceiving of public schooling as the source of the political capacity essential to the health of a free society has proved a chimera.[86] Inevitably the schools are caught in the maelstrom of modern politics. The radical critique pictures the schools principally as agencies of social control, as instrumentalities imparting attitudes and values compatible with the interests of the rich and powerful. The response from the Right does not so much deny the social-control purposes of public education as to complain that those purposes are being inadequately served by the schools.[87]

For those whose experience with public elementary and secondary schools antedated the early 1960s, however, the most startling aspect of modern attitudes is the widespread loss in the aspirations and expectations held for public education.[88] The buoyant confidence in the social capacities of public education expressed by Horace Mann in 1849, was until recently shared in some measure by most Americans:

> Our ambition, as a State, should . . . [encompass] the solution of such problems as these: To what extent can competence displace pauperism? How nearly can we free ourselves from the low-minded and the vicious; not by their expatriation, but by their elevation? To what extent can the resources and powers of nature be converted into human welfare; the peaceful arts of life be advanced, and the vast treasures of human talent and genius be developed? How much of suffering, in all its forms, can be relieved; or, what is better than relief, how much can be prevented? Cannot the classes of crimes be lessened, and the numbers of criminals, in each class, be diminished?[89]

Clearly, for Horace Mann, public education was to play the leading role in achieving these ends. The contrast with modern attitudes could hardly be more complete. In the decade just past one of the debates concerning public education posed the question of whether the system could reasonably be expected to graduate high-school students possessed of basic literacy. Statements of some school officials warned against a too precipitate pursuit of that objective.[90] Research conducted in recent years underscores the losses in aspirations for public education. One study reports that what is actually learned in school has relatively little to do with the kind of school attended, that increases in school expenditures are not likely to increase academic achievement nor redistribution of resources to reduce inequalities in achievement, and that reforms in education will not contribute significantly to social changes outside the schools.[91] To the question of what aspirations can then be reasonably held for public education, the answer given is that the schools may be expected to provide an environment as safe and healthful as possible for the children who spend up to a quarter of their lives there, an environment that produces a minimum of misery and boredom.[92] Schools are seen "primarily as selection and certification agencies, whose job is to measure and label people and only secondarily as socialization agencies, whose job is to change people."[93] Other and more hopeful estimates of the schools' functions and capacities persist in American society. Nevertheless, accompanying the decline of the rehabilitative ideal in the 1970s is a pervasive loss of confidence in public education as an instrument of human malleability.

In exploring the cultural context of the rehabilitative ideal in the 1970s, attention must eventually be directed to the institutions and practices of therapy outside the penal system. The situation encountered is complex and the evidence it supplies is not easily interpreted. There are many indications of substantial losses of confidence in the capacities and motives underlying traditional programs of behavior alteration and guidance. Part of the new skepticism is a product of political movements that arose in the 1960s attacking exercises of authority in almost all historical forms. One of the tendencies of the Vietnam era was to view the practice of psychiatry as a mode of social control. Two prominent war resisters in those years advised their imprisoned colleagues "to steer clear of the Mental Hygiene Clinic."[94] Radical politics eschewed a psychology of personal adjustment as a ruse to distract attention from the necessary overturning of social institutions.[95] The new ideology created consternation in some practitioners of the helping professions, leaving traditional assumptions in those disciplines in considerable disarray. Some of the modern skepticism, while perhaps influenced by political ideology, is less directly related to it. Organizations of mental hospital patients, former patients, and others, have been formed challenging certain procedures of institutional treatment such as shock therapy and certain kinds of drug therapy.[96] Another form of skepticism, widely dispersed in American society and often expressed in legal circles, has origins dating well before the past decade. One of the important checks on government activism in cases of alleged emotional neglect of children and even child abuse, are strong and persisting doubts about the capacities of the helping professions to manage interventions into family situations that actually advance the welfare of children intended to be helped.[97]

Yet the manifestations of increasing skepticism of institutional therapeutic programs constitute considerably less than half the picture. Accompanying these losses in confidence and the decline of the rehabilitative ideal in penal justice has been the rise of a new psychologism, a phenomenon of such magnitude that it can fairly be identified as one of the principal characteristics of contemporary American society. Evidences of the new psychologism abound. These include the millions of persons now or recently undergoing traditional forms of therapy and the great increase in the numbers of psychiatrists and parapsychiatrists trained and in practice since World War II.[98] These statistics, however, constitute only a small part of the reality. They do not include the millions committed to less traditional therapeutic programs operated by persons of greatly varying training, credentials, and credibility.[99] There are presumably millions more practicing their own regimes of life changing and self-awareness under the guidance of the authors of a popular psychological literature that engulfs the book stands. "Therapeutic man" is inescapable in modern America. He pervades television talk shows and situation comedies and is expressed in commercial advertising, popular music, and the other popular arts. The new psychologism has gone far to transform issues formerly defined as problems of education, morals, and politics into occasions for therapeutic diagnosis and manipulation.[100] American society (to use Professor Delgadeo's unattractive term) has become "psychocivilized."[101] These phenomena, at least on first view, appear to disclose a high confidence in human malleability in contemporary American society, a confidence difficult to reconcile with the decline of the rehabilitative ideal in criminal justice.

One seeking to understand the juxtaposition of these two developments must direct attention to certain characteristics of the new psychologism. In much of it, one discovers an extreme anti-intellectual orientation. Thus the founder of gestalt therapy wrote: "Each time you ask the question *why*, you diminish in stature. You bother yourself with false, unnecessary information. You only feed the computer, the intellect. . . . It's a drag on your life."[102] The impact of the new psychologism on the life of universities and on the possibilities of achieving social purposes through rational policy formulation can hardly be insignificant.

For the purposes at hand, however, there is another aspect of the new psychologism of greater importance: the sense of dependency in American society that it reveals and exploits. Unlike the self-improvement efforts typical of American life in the last century, the present phenomenon discloses no sturdy individualism. It does not constitute a rebirth of what our fathers called "republican virtue" with its emphasis on both public purposes and individual autonomy.[103] Expressions of the loss of autonomy in contemporary society to experts and the regimes they prescribe are sometimes bizarre. Recently a national television series announced that on its next showing viewers would receive expert counsel on how to enjoy their vacations. The flood of misery suffered that summer by those who unfortunately missed the show can easily be imagined. The impulse to place oneself in relations of subservience and dependency to those performing therapeutic or religious rituals may suggest more somber implications. Edward O. Wilson speaks of "the masochistic relief that results from placing oneself into the hands of the master to whom omnipotence has been granted."[104] These propensities of the new psychologism demand sympathetic consideration, for, however vulnerable to caricature, they point to conditions important for social thought and action. The sense of dependency manipulated by the new psychologism reflects the reality of dependency in social, economic, and political realms. The loss of public purpose must express a sense of impotence in the public arena. One suspects that the movement toward self as the source, object, and measure of all satisfaction is related to a loss of confidence in the ability of individuals to affect social outcomes or to affect them for the better. As others have observed, however, the movement represents less than an exaltation of self. It has not generally nourished the autonomy of individuals but has expressed a weariness with selfhood.[105]

The dominant assumptions of much in the new psychologism are radically different from those manifested in traditional applications of the rehabilitative ideal. Whatever deficiencies in concept and execution may be attributed to American rehabilitationism, it is, after all, dedicated to the achievement of social purposes. It seeks, most importantly, to strengthen the social defense against criminal acts by eliminating or lessening criminal recidivism. Insofar as the rehabilitative ideal undertakes to advance the interests and satisfactions of offenders, it does so by efforts intended to bring the offenders' behavior and attitudes into harmony with certain values socially defined and validated. In this sense the rehabilitative ideal takes its stand on the side of character, on the development of internal controls attuned to the achievement of personal and social goals. No comparable social orientation characterizes much of the popular psychologism. On the contrary, its typical emphasis is on comfort, solace, self-awareness, escape from pain and responsibility. There is a curious identity between the concepts of "character disorder" and "psychopathic personality" in the older psychiatric literature and the picture of "therapeutic man" drawn by Philip Reiff over a decade ago.[106] The picture is one of persons who respond directly to instinctual drives inhibited as little as possible by cultural "demand systems," whose ultimate goals are personal satisfaction, who are largely uninfluenced by social purposes or the interests of other individuals except as the latter may contribute to personal self-realization.[107] The reliances on human malleability in the new psychologism are sharply distinguishable from those expressed in the rehabilitative ideal, and this fact explains not only why the rise of the new psychologism is compatible with the decline of penal rehabilitationism, but also why it has been an important factor in that decline.

There is ample evidence, then, that modern views of human malleability and confidence in traditional institutions to effect socially desirable direction to human behavior and aspirations are not those of earlier periods of American history when the rehabilitative ideal first clearly emerged and flourished. Many of the same factors that have conditioned contemporary views about human malleability operate to obstruct a modern consensus on the goals of rehabilitation. When therapy is administered by a system of penal justice, the ends of therapy inevitably become matters of social concern and definition, however dedicated the individual therapist may be to the proposition that the goals of treatment are ultimately matters of choice for the patient.[108] Yet there are few more difficult problems for a pluralistic society than to achieve agreement on what rehabilitation consists of, or when cure has been achieved. Sometimes these disagreements are overt and raucous. One of the many controversies surrounding the practice of drastic therapies like lobotomy and other forms of psychosurgery involves the application of the labels "cured" or "improved" to some whose conditions after such procedures seem hardly to justify these optimistic descriptions.[109] There are more important obstacles to consensus, however. Perhaps the most significant of these are the modern disputes concerning what behavior is to be made subject to criminal penalties; for if agreement cannot be reached on what acts are to be proscribed, consensus will be lacking on what it means to be rehabilitated. Contemporary efforts, often strongly resisted, to decriminalize offenses involving private sexual behavior, the uses of alcohol and other drugs, gambling, and the like, reflect not a search for consensus so much as a recognition of its absence.[110] One of the arresting aspects of the current abortion controversy is its demonstration of the extraordinary divisions in American society on what it means to be a criminal. Less dramatic but hardly less important are the controversies over the elimination of status offenses from juvenile-court jurisdiction.[111] Even in the areas of violent criminality there is disagreement on what it means to be a criminal and hence what it means to be rehabilitated. The written law's efforts to limit the uses of deadly force in cases involving self-defense and the protection of property and habitation are often frustrated by those in the community who adhere to an ethic of private violence. Sharply conflicting views on political violence and terrorism illustrate a similar condition.[112]

American society in the 1970s fails to satisfy the cultural conditions necessary for a flourishing rehabilitative ideal. Fundamental explanation of its precipitous decline in this decade requires resort to cultural events whose origins lie well outside the system of penal justice. Events and conditions touching criminal law administration more directly, however, have also played a role in the decline of the rehabilitative ideal. Perceptions of increasing crime in the late 1960s brought with them a heightened sense of insecurity and fears of a collapse of public order. These perceptions were based in part on demographic realities. In the quarter of a century following 1950, the number of males fifteen to seventeen years of age doubled in the United States, a fact of great significance for many areas of public policy. For criminal justice it meant the rapid enlargement of those segments of the population in which much serious crime is most frequently committed.[113] Fears of increasing crime have long constituted a powerful dynamic in American politics, and as experience in both Britain and America attests, provide an unfavorable climate for the rehabilitative ideal.[114]

Other factors have been at work. Hostility to authority engendered by the civil rights movement and resistance to the Vietnam War; the tendency of some black activists to equate criminal sanctions with political oppression; and the Watergate experience—all struck at the roots of penal rehabilitationism. A sucessful rehabilitative program requires a perception of its legitimacy, both in the public that authorizes it and also in the subjects of the program. Among both groups, and particularly in the second, this sense of legitimacy has weakened. Matching the suspicions and skepticism of those subjected to rehabilitative efforts is a growing public pessimism about the capacities of penal programs to achieve reform. This pessimism requires further analysis, but there is reason to suspect that in part it is related to a widespread perception of the American crime problem as one principally of race. It is hardly coincidental that the decline in public support for the rehabilitative ideal accompanies rising percentages of noncaucasian inmates in the prisons.[115] Optimism about the possibilities of reform flourishes when strong bonds of identity are perceived between the reformers and those to be reformed. Conversely, confidence in rehabilitative effort dwindles when a sense of difference and social distance separates the promoters from the subjects of reform.[116] A curious illustration of this is the extraordinary pessimism expressed in antebellum America about the reform of female prisoners. The pessimism had its roots in perceptions of radical differences between males and females. Woman was seen as made of purer and more refined material. When she fell into criminal ways, therefore, she fell from a greater height, and rescaling the slope was for her correspondingly more difficult.[117] "The gulf that separates men from insects," wrote the novelist Charles Brockden Brown, "is not wider than that which severs the polluted from the chaste among women."[118] Conceiving of crime as principally the product of the "criminal classes" or of criminal justice as a war between the "peace forces" and the "criminal forces" is antagonistic to sincere reformism. Yet these perceptions are prominent leitmotifs of the 1970s.

Penal theory in the United States and the Western world in this century has often appeared parochial—formalistic in its statements and only partially aware of the principal currents of thought and events outside the areas of its immediate concerns. A greater consciousness of these matters, however, does not itself resolve the problems of policy formulation for the remainder of the twentieth century. The strategies of reform may be enhanced by awareness of the impact of the modern malaise on penal rehabilitationism. Yet critical questions remain. A thoroughgoing modern critique of the rehabilitative ideal underlies much of the contemporary reform movement in the criminal law. What is the nature of the critique and what is its validity? What problems have emerged in programs of reform founded on the rejection of rehabilitationism, and what role, if any, should the rehabilitative ideal play in the future? These questions provide themes for the chapters that follow.

T W O

The Rehabilitative Ideal and
Its Modern Critics

The history of the rehabilitative ideal constitutes a kind of thematic counterpoint of aspirations and doubts. Criticisms of penal rehabilitationism attended its birth. There was no initial period when enthusiasm for the reform of prisoners wholly overcame criticism and skepticism. On the contrary, one finds in antebellum America the same questions being raised that figure in the modern critique of the rehabilitative ideal: Are offenders capable of redemption? Are the methods employed in rehabilitative efforts adequate to achieve the ends of reformation? Do the techniques of rehabilitation threaten basic political values by overstepping the bounds of fair procedure and ignoring proper limits on state intervention? At present, as in the past, understanding the rehabilitative ideal requires that careful attention be given to its critics. As was noted in the first chapter, the modern decline of penal rehabilitationism cannot be fully explained by the persuasiveness of the logical cases arrayed against it. Yet the criticisms are important, for in them may be found the assumptions on which contemporary efforts to recast criminal justice are based. Some modern reactions present very little of intellectual interest; they comprise essentially irritated responses to the prevalence of crime and offer only an all-encompassing faith in the efficacy of coercion and repression. Such a characterization, however, is in no way descrip-

tive of the views of many who today oppose the rehabilitative ideal. The latter are troubled by the political implications of penal rehabilitationism and are sensitive to the
conflicts built into a system of criminal justice that seeks to
express simultaneously the values of human responsibility
and the reform of offenders.[1] Accordingly, attention needs to
be given to the modern critique of the rehabilitative ideal.

The modern case against the rehabilitative ideal has been in
the making at least since the years immediately preceding
World War II. It derives from a variety of sources and was
largely formulated before political movements in the late
1960s appropriated it for their own purposes. Among its important sources were American attitudes toward the rise of
European totalitarian regimes in the years following the First
World War. The perversions of criminal justice to the ends of
dictatorial governments led many observers to the conviction
that containment of political power exerted within penal systems is an indispensable part of the strategy of freedom.[2]
This conviction underlay the burgeoning of the American
constitutional law of criminal procedure, and the same perception led some critics to challenge what were thought to be
the political assumptions of the rehabilitative ideal. Even
more explicit political concerns were voiced by certain social
theorists. Some writers perceived the methodology of penal
treatment, including that ostensibly directed to rehabilitative
ends, as essentially a product of social structure and the dynamics of Western industrial society.[3] Other commentators
associated modern rehabilitationism with psychiatric theory
and were disposed to doubt the capacities of psychiatric technique to achieve penal reform and sometimes challenged the
intellectual foundations of psychiatric science.[4] Although the
critics shared no common fund of assumptions, the modern
critique of the rehabilitative ideal appears to rest on three
principal propositions. First, the rehabilitative ideal consti-

tutes a threat to the political values of free societies.[5] Second—a distinct but closely related point—the rehabilitative ideal has revealed itself in practice to be peculiarly vulnerable to debasement and the serving of unintended and unexpressed social ends. Third, either because of scientific ignorance or institutional incapacities, a rehabilitative technique is lacking; we do not know how to prevent criminal recidivism by changing the characters and behavior of offenders. Each of these points will be examined in turn.

To the social theorist, perhaps the most striking feature of much twentieth-century discussion of penal rehabilitationism is the absence of explicit political analysis.[6] In 1959 a prominent American psychiatrist published a popular article entitled "Verdict Guilty—Now What?"[7] The title expressed the characteristic emphasis of much midcentury criminological literature. Concerns were focused on the encounter between the convicted prisoner and the therapist or the therapeutic program. The propriety of the prisoner's conviction was assumed, and political issues associated with the definitions of crime and the apprehension, trial, and commitment of offenders were ignored or slighted. The possibilities of malicious or even mistaken uses of power in rehabilitative programs were rarely adverted to, revealing a largely unquestioned reliance on the therapist's dedication to science and to his professionalism as sufficient guarantees against abuses of authority.[8] Oddly enough, much American literature dealing with the treatment of convicted offenders preserved its innocence of political comment at a time when such concerns were animating the emerging constitutional law of criminal procedure. Even some members of the Supreme Court, however, were slow to perceive the kinship of the political issues that pervade the guilt-determining process and those that emerge in the treatment process.[9]

The neglect of the political context of criminal justice by some of the twentieth-century votaries of the rehabilitative ideal could not indefinitely characterize criminological thought in postwar America. Indeed there is reason to conclude that the apolitical posture of some penal reformists was itself a matter of considerable political significance. Thus the medical model of crime correction, the notion that the key to domestic tranquillity lies in the confrontation between therapist and prisoner, may prove attractive to those disinclined to implicate existing social arrangements in the causes and virulence of American crime and reluctant to concede the necessity for social change.[10] However this may be, the case for a political analysis of criminal justice in the postwar world became irresistible. Such an analysis is compatible with much in the American legal tradition. The structure of restraints imposed on governmental authority by the federal Bill of Rights and similar provisions in state constitutions reflected an acute sense of the political implications of criminal justice and a realistic appraisal of seventeenth-century English experience with the criminal law as an instrument of royal power.

In the years that followed the generation of the Founding Fathers, however, little systematic attention was directed to the political dimensions of criminal justice in the United States. The absence of serious political oppression in the American past militated against a concept of political crime, a concept that flourished on the Continent and was a product of nineteenth-century European liberalism.[11] Although American history is interspersed with sporadic expressions of alarm and resentment about the "crime problem," until recently there has been no strong or consistent tendency to relate the epidemic of crime to the functioning of American social and political institutions. Instead, crime has been seen most typically as an aberration and as the product of weaknesses of individual character or of the propensities of various ethnic and racial groups.[12] An analysis of criminal justice in political terms is most likely to emerge in a society whose basic political and social assumptions are in doubt and contention. The apolitical character of American attitudes, including those revealed by penal rehabilitationists in mid-twentieth century, reflects a high degree of consensus on underlying political assumptions, a consensus that, despite the emphasis of some modern revisionist historians, has characterized the dominant and articulate elements of American society for most of its history.

The decade of the 1960s witnessed a considerable erosion of the American consensus and an increasing tendency toward political interpretations of criminal justice. The immediate reasons are clear. Large numbers of Americans, including many born in affluent and influential segments of the population, found themselves in adamant opposition to governmental policy in southeastern Asia, and some of these became the objects of criminal prosecution. A rising racial militancy and attrition between the generations produced similar confrontations. Those committed to uncompromising opposition to public policy and for that reason in jeopardy of penal sanctions, will almost inevitably see criminal justice as the interest of the stronger, as an exercise of social control devoid of moral authority. Such a stance explains to the resister the precarious situation in which he finds himself and provides ethical justification for his conduct to which the state affixes the label of illegality.[13] These interpretations of the criminal process were by no means confined to the antiwar activists. A large and sympathetic segment of the community accepted the same definitions, and in the universities strands of social theory that had been long in incubation and reflected similar perceptions were invigorated by the cultural and political events of the 1960s.

Political interpretations of criminal justice, once launched, found sustenance both in the facts of the twentieth-century world and also in an older literary and historical tradition. The facts that the criminal law expresses state policy and that its enforcement is a state function directed to the achievement of politically defined goals cannot be doubted; and it may be inferred that the administration of criminal justice will in general serve, or at least not seriously disserve, the apparent interests of those capable of influencing public policy and its implementation. Although these propositions are fundamental to any modern analysis, they are also very nearly tautological and seem hardly to warrant the excitement they have engendered in recent years.

One may also expect that the same forces that move and give shape to the larger society will affect the nature and operations of criminal justice and that penal reformers will express culturally generated attitudes toward human nature, property relations, and political and religious obligation. These points have been frequently elaborated in modern historical literature. The prison, especially, has been subjected to political scrutiny. Writers have asserted that the penitentiary movement in antebellum America had significance going much beyond the immediate concerns of crime control, that the prison with its regime of hard labor and strict discipline was seen as a model for the larger society, and that the penal reforms reflected the hopes and particularly the fears of Jacksonian reformers, some of whom foresaw anarchy as the consequence of the unprecedented American experiment in political democracy.[14] The tendency of modern social theory to formulate political interpretations is buttressed by a literary consciousness that employs the prison as a metaphor for modern society.[15] This is not a new tradition. It was expressed in Charles Dickens's *Little Dorrit*[16] as well as in the more recent somber morality play of Ken Kesey, *One Flew Over the Cuckoo's Nest*.[17] It may be seen in its most explicit forms in apocalyptic utopias like Zamiatin's *We*, Huxley's *Brave New World*, and Orwell's *1984*, which, respectively, portray political applications of psychosurgery, biological engineering, and aversion therapy.[18]

Political interpretations of criminal justice are characteristic and inevitable products of the present age of politics. More than this, however, is the fact that an accurate sense of the potential of criminal justice as an instrumentality for the destruction of basic political values is essential in these times to the survival of liberal societies. Yet the increasing modern tendency to focus criminological attention on the political dimensions of criminal justice is attended with certain dangers and inconveniences. The notion that criminal justice is simply the interest of the stronger is essentially a revolutionary idea. Any functioning political society relies on the perception that all classes in the community have a stake in public order. One of the basic tactics of the criminal law is to create categories of criminality bearing lesser political weight: categories of "private" homicides, assaults, and thefts. This may, of course, be denounced as a "stratagem of social control"; but its justification is that it makes possible the imposition of smaller quantums of force in criminal law administration. One reason totalitarian regimes often require overwhelming force to maintain acceptable levels of public order is the tendency of such regimes to translate criminal deviance into political criminality, into forms of treason.[19]

The dangers to a liberal polity arising from the tendency to view criminal justice largely in political terms is amply illustrated by recent American history. For a time in the late 1960s both the government and some who were made objects of penal scrutiny largely accepted political definitions of the criminal process. The "war against crime" trumpeted by successive national administrations and coming to dubious climax in the Nixon era, projected an image of incipient civil war. It was a posture that emphasized dangers of social and political collapse, relegating to secondary importance all other issues of penal policy including even concerns about personal security threatened by widespread criminality.[20] At the same time, large and potentially powerful groups in American society began to perceive ordinary forms of criminality as a kind of political protest against poverty and oppression, thereby enhancing the possibility of more intense and overt applications of the public force in response. Liberal regimes are vulnerable when such escalations of force are or appear to be required. Their liberal character is imperiled by practices of continuing large-scale repression.

A second inconvenience associated with modern political interpretations of criminal justice are the current uses of criminological theory as an instrumentality of politics. Such uses of course are not new. Theories about the causes of crime and the treatment of offenders express views about the nature of human beings and society and are, in some sense, both a product and handmaiden of politics. This has always been true, yet one wonders whether in the American universities there has ever been such overt conscription of criminological theory to the interests of political ideology as at present. What has come to be known as the social control school provides one, but only one, illustration of the tendency.[21] Much of the writing displays high intellectual capacity, and some of it provides knowledge and insights of value to readers of widely differing political orientations. Even at its best, however, the argument is often tendentious and reductive. In general, an effort is made to incorporate social deviance and the repressive responses of the bourgeois society into a much broader theory of social dynamics. Presumably many of the writers are in substantial accord with Mao's observation that "the state apparatus, including the army, the police and the courts, is the instrumentality by which one class oppresses another."[22] There is a tendency toward the sweeping generalization inadequately disciplined by empirical demonstration. Thus Michel Foucault appears to assert that bourgeois society deliberately creates crime both in order to justify a law-enforcement mechanism quickly adaptable to the suppression of political dissent and also to divert the more aggressive members of the dispossessed classes into the commission of ordinary crimes and away from revolutionary action against the dominant social interests.[23] Because it is macrotheory that is being written, the significance of individual motivation and action tends to be ignored or underestimated.[24] The portrayal of the great penal reformers is especially suspect. Religious motives are rarely taken seriously or adequately understood.[25] At its worst, the literature descends into a series of political "just so" tales reflecting little of the historical reality it purports to convey and seeking to create a usable past, usable for contemporary and future revolutionary politics. Ultimately the question raised by these extravagances is whether criminology retains a function in the late twentieth century. Is the effort to ameliorate the administration of criminal justice futile and indefensible; does it simply reinforce for a season the expiring power of a tyrannical capitalist society?

It is not surprising to discover that in the present intellectual climate, critiques of the rehabilitative ideal focus strongly on its political implications. Despite the limitations of such analysis, it is important that this scrutiny should proceed. It requires no great penetration to discern that modern controversies surrounding penal rehabilitationism are in significant degree debates about human nature. "Who will deny," asked Isaiah Berlin, "that political problems . . . depend logically and directly on what man's nature is taken to be?"[26] Nor can it be denied that conflicting theories of crime causation and penal treatment also rest ultimately on opposing perceptions of human character and potential. It is this circumstance that most clearly identifies issues of penal policy with the larger political controversies of the time.[27]

In the past century and a half American scientific and humanistic literatures have displayed a bewildering array of theories relating to crime and punishment.[28] Some of these were indigenous to American society; most were borrowed from European sources and applied to local circumstances. No simple classification can adequately portray the diversity of their assumptions and emphases. It is useful for present purposes, however, to conceive of this agglomeration of theories as clustering about two opposing poles: one conceiving of deviant behavior as importantly influenced or determined by heritable biological factors; the other viewing behavior as largely the product of culture and other environmental causes. The nature-nurture controversy waxed hotly in the United States in the fifty years following 1880 and has lately been revived—one hopes in somewhat more sophisticated guise—in the recent debates on sociobiology.[29]

Among the most characteristic expressions of nineteenth-century thought were the efforts made, for better or worse, to give immediate social application to the new knowledge proliferating in the biological sciences. In the areas of crime and punishment a plethora of theories emerged: phrenology, criminal anthropology with its concept of the "born criminal," notions of degeneracy, atavism, and constitutional incapacities of offenders to adapt to human society.[30] By all odds, the most important of these phenomena was the eugenics movement, which for the first three decades of the present century rivaled the rehabilitative ideal in its appeal to the educated and influential segments of the community.[31] The political and social implications of theories stressing biological factors in the causes and treatment of crime were not always clear. The eugenics movement became part of the program of Progressive reform in the early decades of this century and received the support of persons of widely differing political commitments. Moreover, the relations of scientific theories to political convictions are often anything but obvious and straightforward, a fact sometimes overlooked in simplistic social analysis. Nevertheless, the political coloration of the eugenics movement became more apparent as time went on. The notion that crime, poverty, and other kinds of personal misfortune are largely products of heritable biological mechanisms suggested the futility of social reforms other than those

promoting selective human breeding. Certainly the rehabilitative ideal with its strong environmental assumptions was regarded as suspect.[32] The concepts of biological superiority
and inferiority when transported to the political arena proved
incompatible with egalitarian aspirations, and many leading
figures in the eugenics movement expressed strongly anti-
democratic sentiments.[33] Even more somber were assertions
of the inferiority of races other than those contributing to
north European stock.[34] In short, the eugenics movement, or
many of its adherents, employed the fact of human diversity
as an explanation for political and economic inequalities and
as a defense for existing systems of privilege.

This observation, of course, does not challenge the legitimacy of scientific inquiry into the biological bases of human
behavior, nor does it imply that those advancing genetic ex-
planations of social deviance are engaged in an unworthy vin-
dication of the status quo. Yet this chapter of American intellectual history needs to be pondered. Any stance toward
complex social issues has its own characteristic forms of pathology and perversion. It is important that these tendencies
be known so that their more disastrous consequences can be
avoided. The obscenities of Nazi racial policy provide an almost too vivid demonstration of the pathologies of crude
biologism. It is worthwhile to recall, however, that even Nazi
racism provided an intellectual attraction for some young
men. The third-ranking medical doctor in the German state
hierarchy testified that he joined the party on perceiving that
"Nazism is applied biology."[35]

The perversions of biological theories of human behavior
remain strong in the public consciousness, particularly in
those persons espousing radical social reform. It is not
difficult to understand why this should be true. The assumption of human malleability is central to programs of far-
reaching social reconstruction. Such programs necessarily
assume that drastic alterations in both individual and

institutional behavior are possible, that present woes have their sources not in the genes, but in a corrupt social system.[36] Faith in human malleability, of course, is not confined to radical reformers. On the contrary, it in some degree characterizes most modern men and women and provides the assumption on which much social behavior rests. Among the groups most committed to the possibilities of human malleability are the penal rehabilitationists. In this respect they share the assumptions of radical reformers, however much they may differ with them on goals and methods. What political activists and rehabilitationists sometimes overlook, however, is that extreme environmentalism, an unquestioned confidence in the malleability of human nature, also tends to its own distinctive forms of perversion. Moreover, these perversions are as destructive of liberal political values as those associated with theories of biological determinism. Indeed, it is difficult to conceive of any intellectual stance more hostile to those values than the assumption of complete malleability of human nature expressed in Russian and, especially, Chinese social theory.[37] For if an idyllic human condition is within the capacities of organized society, if thoughts and deeds of individuals can be conditioned to achieve some all-encompassing harmony that realizes the full possibilities of human existence, then those possessed of political power may be morally mandated to subject the most intimate aspects of human life to extreme state interventions. Concepts of human freedom and dignity are threads too fragile to contain policy founded on such assumptions.[38]

The notion of the total malleability of human nature has not dominated the thoughts and attitudes of Western societies. A typical Western conception of an essentially unvarying human nature located against the constantly shifting backdrop of history was sardonically expressed by the novelist John Galsworthy, who when musing on the just-ended reign of Queen Victoria, reflected that it was "a great Age, whose transmuting influence nothing has escaped save the nature of man and the nature of the Universe."[39] The notion of there being basic attributes of human nature that may be modified but not eradicated lies near the center of the Western liberal tradition. This view asserts that there is an essential human nature that persists in time and across cultural boundaries and implies that there are some things that society and its agencies cannot achieve and ought not to undertake. Statements of the position abound in American political thought. Thus in 1824 James Madison is found saying "Let it be remembered . . . that the rights [America] contended were the rights of human nature."[40] That a nucleus of biological attributes provides a shield for individuals against the aggressions of civilization and hence is an aspect of human freedom, was asserted by Sigmund Freud. "It does not seem as though any influence," he wrote, "could induce a man to change his nature into a termite's."[41] From an entirely different perspective Erving Goffman described the defeat by inmates in total institutions of efforts to determine their behavior. These "homely little histories, each in its way a movement of liberty" he reduced to a proposition: "Whenever worlds are laid on, underlives develop."[42]

The liberal political stance and penal rehabilitationism coexist in a continuing state of tension, even though the resulting unease is more acutely sensed in some periods than in others. Ronald Dworkin, addressing a much broader range of issues, has remarked, "The liberal is concerned to expand imagination without imposing any particular choice upon imagination."[43] From the liberal perspective, any system of penal regulation, however oriented, is at best a necessary evil—the necessity stemming from the presence in the community of those who unjustifiably subvert the interests and volition of other persons. The movement from penal incapacitation of offenders to their reform, however, introduces a new order of concerns; for efforts to influence by coercive means the very thoughts, feelings, and aspirations of offenders threaten trespass by the state upon areas of dignity and choice posited as immune by the liberal creed. One reason the tension between liberalism and the rehabilitative ideal has not always been seen as critical is that the means often employed in rehabilitative efforts have been such that, if at all successful, they require a considerable voluntary cooperative effort on the part of the subject.[44] When, however, the rehabilitative effort moves from the use of devices like those of traditional psychotherapy to what have been called the extreme therapies—pyschosurgery, aversive conditioning, and certain other forms of behavioral modification—the state employs rehabilitative techniques that typically impose feelings and perceptions on the subject that in a meaningful sense are not of his own making, techniques that one observer describes as "manipulating people inside the perimeter of their conscious defenses."[45] The liberal unease with such forms of rehabilitation reflects, not a Luddite rejection of scientific "advance," but rather an awareness that they constitute incursions by the state into areas of human freedom and autonomy believed to lie outside the proper province of state action.

The principles of consent and voluntarism derived from liberal political values suggest certain limitations on the methods that may legitimately be employed in rehabilitative efforts. The widespread disregard of these limitations, both in this country and around the world, constitutes one of the serious modern complaints about penal rehabilitationism. The limitations contemplate two sorts of voluntarism. There is, first, consent to the initiation of the behavior-changing program. The difficulties surrounding the implementation of informed consent have been widely discussed and need not be detailed here.[46] They involve subtleties and ambiguities that in some degree pervade any relation of therapist and subject and are immeasurably complicated when the consent sought is one from an inmate in a total institution.[47] There is, however, a second kind of voluntarism that involves not only a meaningful assent to the initiation of the rehabilitative effort, but also a continuing consent and a continuing effort on the part of the subject, which make behavorial changes as they occur his personal achievements. Acceptance of the principles of consent and voluntarism provides at least a modicum of meaning to the aspect of the rehabilitative ideal asserting that penal treatment should result in benefit to the offender. When what is good for the offender is exclusively determined by the state or, as is often the case, by state functionaries able to escape effective public scrutiny and control, destructive consequences are likely to follow. Lines between therapy and repression tend to fade. One of the striking ironies of American history is the emergence of regimes of virtual slavery in the antebellum prisons in Auburn and Sing Sing, regimes motivated at the outset by rehabilitative objectives and defended as providing useful lessons in diligence and labor.[48] This and more recent proposals for the use of psychosurgery as a cure for the violence displayed in northern ghetto riots illustrate what may be lost by neglect of the principle of voluntarism.[49] Even when dramatic outcomes are avoided, such neglect may result in the infantilization of adults and in losses of autonomy and human dignity.[50]

The political implications of the rehabilitative ideal, however, encompass far more than the kinds of rehabilitative techniques employed. Regardless of the means applied, a range of problems emerge involving control of the discretion of public agencies, and these problems have proved persistent and disturbing.[51] The issues are among the most frequently discussed in the recent legal literature on corrections. The attention given them by lawyers and judges has resulted in new applications of due process doctrine such as those relating to the procedures of juvenile courts and to the concept of prisoners' rights.[52] No reprise of this voluminous literature is required, but the reasons issues of discretion arise and judicial doctrine has as yet imperfectly resolved them are entitled to brief consideration.

Therapeutic theories of penal treatment have often conceived of crime as symptomatic of an affliction, but the nature of the disease and how it differs from other pathologies are generally obscure.[53] Vagueness in the conception of the disorder is communicated, in turn, to thought about its cure. Much of the political unease engendered by this version of the rehabilitative ideal stems from its central conception. One immediate consequence of a rehabilitative regime is a drastic enlargement of state concerns. The state's interests now embrace not only the offender's conduct, but, as Michel Foucault has put it, his "soul": his motives, his history, his social environment.[54] A traditional restraint on governmental authority is the notion of relevance: the state is limited in its inquiries and actions to that which is pertinent to its legitimate purposes. But when there are no clear limits on what may be relevant to the treatment process and when the goals of treatment have not been clearly defined, the idea of relevance as a regulator of public authority is destroyed or impaired.[55]

There is abundant evidence of basic incompatibilities between the adversary system of criminal justice and at least some manifestations of the rehabilitative ideal. A leading proponent of penal rehabilitationism has rightly observed, "There will come a point at which a personal approach and the 'educational atmosphere' of good will and cooperation would be frustrated, if prisoner and official regarded their mutual relationship only from the strict legal point of view."[56] The tension between rights and treatment, however, often reveals itself in stages of the process that antedate the prison therapeutic program and penetrates even the guilt-determining process. When a group in England called for enlargement of the therapeutic approach to penal corrections, the reflex of a police spokesman was instantaneous. That approach, he said, "ought to allow a change in the procedure of investigation and trial so as to enable the truth or, if you like, the diagnosis to be more easily established."[57] The assumption of benevolent purpose in penal regimes with strong rehabilitative bents sometimes undermines systems of criminal procedure based on the conception of individual rights. The willingness of the accused to assert adversary positions against the state may be taken as the strongest evidence of the accused's need of rehabilitation. It is said that wise political prisoners in the People's Republic of China understand that insistence on their legal rights of appeal often results in more, rather than less, enforced "political education"; for such insistence is viewed by the authorities as an expression of the very attitudes that the rehabilitative regime is intended to alter or suppress.[58] The high importance accorded full confessions of guilt in the Chinese system likewise reveals the conclusion that the affliction most in need of cure is the propensity of individuals to fend off the benevolent embrace of state power. The Chinese case is a stark and no doubt extreme instance of these tendencies, but one who has observed the operations of juvenile courts in this country and has noted the hostility displayed in some to adversary procedures and the large significance attached to confessions of guilt, will not lack for evidence of similar tendencies here.[59]

The assumption of the benevolent purpose of the rehabilitative regime and the highly subjective and ill-defined notions of how rehabilitation is to be achieved and of what it consists, generate other problems. One of these is the tendency of those engaged in rehabilitative efforts to define as therapy anything that a therapist does.[60] Because such disabilities as loss of liberty and other privileges are defined as therapeutic, the officer's sense of self-restraint may be weakened. "It is extremely difficult to hold correctional organizations accountable for the manner in which they execute the powers of the state," Paul Lerman has written, "when they verbally deny that they are involved in a coercive social institution."[61] One consequence, frequently remarked, is the tendency of rehabilitative regimes to inflict larger deprivations of liberty and volition on its subjects than is sometimes exacted from prisoners in more overtly punitive programs.[62]

These, then, constitute part of the catalog of political concerns that have been engendered by the rehabilitative ideal. Whether they or any part of them counsel the total abandonment of penal rehabilitationism or whether it is prudent to persist in rehabilitative efforts if forewarned of their perils, requires further consideration. For the moment, however, it is sufficient to say that the political concerns just discussed take on even greater seriousness when a second broad tendency of the rehabilitative ideal is considered: its tendency in practical application to become debased and to serve other social ends far removed from and sometimes inconsistent with the reform of offenders.

There is no more striking and persistent feature of the history of penal reforms than the tendency of innovations motivated by rehabilitative ends to lose their impetus and efficacy, often within the decade following their initiation.[63] The phenomenon is not confined to the recent history of industrial societies. The Houses of Correction, established in England and on the Continent in the sixteenth and seventeenth centuries, were greeted by contemporaries such as Sir Edward Coke as constructive alternatives to the futility and squalor of the common gaols. By the end of the seventeenth century the Houses were virtually indistinguishable from the gaols.[64] The disappointment of the rehabilitative aspirations of the American penitentiary movement has already been mentioned. In 1867 a legislative report in New York asserted: "There is not a state prison in America in which the reformation of convicts is the one supreme object of the discipline."[65] Similar experiences were duplicated in Britain. A rehabilitative regime of solitary confinement conceived of by its founders as an instrument of penance and correction was being employed a few years later as an effective device for the control of political prisoners.[66] The years following the American Civil War saw the rise of a widely supported reformatory movement in the United States, which resulted in the establishment of the promising institution at Elmira and the articulation of the still-influential *Declaration of Principles* by the Cincinnati correctional congress of 1870.[67] Yet as one observer has written, "The spirit of Cincinnati died with the first generation of humanitarian reformers."[68] Within ten years, wrote another, Elmira "was just another prison."[69] Nor has the tendency toward debasement of rehabilitative policy and practice been confined to institutions of penal justice. Similar progressions characterize the histories of mental hospitals and institutions for children and the needy.[70] These phenomena have proved to be so persistent and universal that serious consideration must be given to the possibility that they reflect something inherent in rehabilitative enterprise.

Understanding the phenomena of debasement is advanced if attention is first directed to the ways in which language has been employed by those initiating and administering programs of penal rehabilitation. What is involved is more than the usual insistence on a technical vocabulary, but rather a marked tendency toward euphemism and obfuscation. The language employed by persons committed to group efforts and institutional goals often reflects institutional purposes and aspirations. This is true whether the organization in which the speaker functions is a university, the military, a political party, or a prison. In some degree the view of reality communicated by such persons will differ from the reality perceived by those lacking similar purposes and commitments. These divergences reflect less the differences in the kinds and amounts of knowledge possessed by the institutional representative than his acceptance of organizational goals and values.

The occurrence, then, is a familiar one and not unique to

penal corrections. What distinguishes the language of rehabilitation is the degree of faith reflected in the efficacy of label changes, the extraordinary gaps between the epithets employed and the commonsense realities that the words are intended to describe, the amorphousness of concepts central to the system of thought.[71] In one place or another solitary confinement has been called "constructive meditation" and a cell for such confinement "the quiet room."[72] Incarceration without treatment of any kind is seen as "milieu therapy" and a detention facility is labeled "Cloud Nine."[73] Disciplinary measures such as the use of cattle prods on inmates become "aversion therapy" and the playing of a powerful fire hose on the backs of recalcitrant adolescents "hydrotherapy."[74] Cell blocks are hospitals, dormitories are wards, latrine cleaning "work therapy."[75] The catalog is almost endless. Some of the euphemisms are conscious distortions of reality and are employed sardonically or with deliberate purpose to deceive. The more serious distortions, however, are those that reflect the self-deception of correctional functionaries. The burgeoning of euphemisms and the insecure grasp on reality that their use often reveals, signal a system of thought and action under extreme pressure. They are symptomatic of factors contributing to the debasement of rehabilitative objectives in practical application.

Central among the causes of debasement is the conceptual weakness of the rehabilitative ideal. Vagueness and ambiguity shroud its most basic suppositions. The ambitious scope and complexity of its agenda make these characteristics comprehensible and perhaps inevitable. They have been apparent to perceptive observers from the earliest periods of American experimentation with penal reform. Thus the young Beaumont and Tocqueville wrote in 1832: "The theories on the reform of prisoners are vague and uncertain. It is not yet known to what degree the wicked may be regenerated, and by what means this regeneration may be obtained."[76]

Ambiguities afflict the very notion of what rehabilitation consists. A consensus on the ends of rehabilitation sufficient to spark movements of penal reform may, however, camouflage wide diversities of orientation that become critical when institutional programs are attempted. The professional staffs of many modern juvenile courts have not resolved, even to their own satisfaction, whether the rehabilitative objective of juvenile justice is the strengthening of the personal autonomy of the adolescent or of his capacities for adjustment to social expectations, or when these goals may be in conflict.

Equally serious is the vagueness that surrounds the means to effect rehabilitation. Much that is most bizarre in the history of penal rehabilitationism stems from scientific ignorance about how changes in the behavior of offenders are to be achieved. The use of the lash at Auburn Prison, Bentham's Panoptican and his corporal punishment machine, and the faith in solitary confinement as a reformative mechanism (to cite only historical examples) testify to deficiencies of knowledge.[77] In general, scientific ignorance has not inspired caution in the devotees of the rehabilitative ideal. On the contrary, the very absence of knowledge has encouraged confident assertions and dogmatic claims. One consequence is the creation of expectations that are inevitably disappointed.[78] As programs fail, euphemisms and pretext burgeon. Among the groups most seriously disenchanted by this cycle are the inmates themselves. A profound obstacle to penal rehabilitation in the contemporary world is the cynicism of the prisoners engendered, at least in part, by such institutional charades.[79]

The weaknesses of concept and technique take on greater significance when it is recognized that even under the most favorable circumstances rehabilitation can never constitute the sole objective of a correctional system, that many other purposes compete with it for realization. Correctional institutions and programs must serve punitive, deterrent, and incapacitative ends. Penal policy must be reconciled with the reality of scarce resources and must not offend too obviously the aspirations and values of the larger society. The rehabilitative ideal has proved itself poorly armed to maintain itself against competing objectives of policy and practice. In consequence, rehabilitative efforts are frustrated, change character, and may ultimately be rejected and abandoned. For an instant in the 1830s the mixed motives of inmate reform, the preservation of established values, the discouragement of crime and the incapacitation of criminals, the maintenance of prison discipline, and the avoidance of burdensome taxation may have seemed capable of harmonious reconciliation. If so, the optimistic expectations did not last long. Very soon these various purposes were often found to be incompatible, and in the competition of values, that of basic reform of the prisoner most often yielded to the force of other objectives.[80] The history of antebellum penal reform has been repeatedly reenacted in the intervening years.

Among the various interests with which the rehabilitative ideal competes are those of the staff and the institution administering the correctional program. System maintenance is frequently confused with inmate reform. Staff positions must be justified, public relations maintained, the media and hostile reform groups kept at arm's length, the demands of political patronage contained.[81] Because rehabilitative programs require an institutional base and because the ends and means of rehabilitation are vague, it is easy to confuse the interests of inmates with those of the institution. These pressures are insidious, in part, because they may contribute to the debasement of the rehabilitative ideal without bad faith in the correctional staff and certainly in the absence of conscious conspiracy to achieve sub-rosa objectives of social control.[82]

Perhaps even more rigorous is the competition between rehabilitation and the punitive and deterrent purposes of penal justice.[83] The rehabilitative ideal is ordinarily outmatched in the struggle. In antebellum America rehabilitative enthusiasm in the penitentiary movement soon abated and a period quickly arrived when inmate reform was accorded only lip service. Ultimately, however, even verbal deference was withheld by many prison officials and some legislative committees, punitive goals were defended, and the objective of reform was denounced as a chimera. The amorphousness of rehabilitative theory and practice contributes to their undoing. It may on occasion be true that the detention or penal incarceration of a young offender, for example, can be defended rationally as serving a rehabilitative end. But given the intensity of the punitive pressures, on the one hand, and the vagueness of rehabilitative criteria, on the other, the temptations to self-deception of correctional personnel in such cases must often prove irresistible.[84] In many instances the latent function of rehabilitative theory is to camouflage punitive measures that might otherwise produce protest in the community. Modern instances abound. While ordinarily described in the language of therapy, the use of aversive techniques on prisoners, such as administering the drug apomorphine to cause vomiting, can hardly be distinguished either in purpose or effect from the cruder forms of corporal punishment once defended as essential to inmate reform.[85] Moreover, lines between therapy, punishment, and institutional control that may appear clear to the institutional staff are often not perceived by the inmate population.

Speculation about the causes of rehabilitative debasement requires that attention be given to the effects of fiscal stringency on both the theory and practice of penal rehabilitation. The effects have been of many sorts. Occasionally in the history of the rehabilitative ideal, penal reformers have displayed a splendid disregard for the fact of scarce resources and an unawareness of insistent competing claims for public support.[86] When taken seriously, such reformers widen even further the gap between expectations and performance in penal programs. More devastating, however, has been the practice of rehabilitationists to seek public support of their agenda by promising savings to taxpayers. Most destructive of all is the tendency to employ the vocabulary of rehabilitation to provide elaborate rationalizations for programs and measures motivated in largest part by fiscal considerations. Although warned against the delusion by the great eighteenth-century reformer John Howard, many early rehabilitationists in the United States believed that the penitentiary system could be made financially self-sufficient and at the same time perform prodigies of inmate reform.[87] The rehabilitative regime established by the People's Republic of China began its career on much the same assumption.[88] In New York the reformers undertook financial commitments so burdensome that they could be borne only through a remarkably harsh system of prison labor. Not surprisingly, the search for institutional profits soon dominated the system. "Because financial considerations were paramount," wrote one historian of the era, "rehabilitation was a mere by-product if it occurred at all. Even the spatial distribution of convict workmen could become penologically harmful if it suited the purposes of a contractor to put a hardened criminal and a youthful offender at the same bench."[89] Laws were eventually passed eliminating or severely restricting systems of contract prison labor, but the motives of such legislation were to eliminate the competition of prison goods and labor from the American market, not to advance inmate reform.[90] The "silent system" of prison management developed in New York in pre-Civil War America overcame the rival ideology of reform through solitary confinement in Pennsylvania because the former proved cheaper to initiate and maintain.[91]

A small treatise could be written on the consequences to penal and welfare policy of efforts to shift expenses of operation from one unit of government to another.[92] Such transfers result not only in the redistribution of costs, but also in important changes in the character and content of the programs. In more than one American jurisdiction, the fact that the costs of probation supervision are borne by local units of government and those of penal incarceration by the state, has profoundly influenced penal dispositions.[93] One need not be wholly skeptical about the virtues of modern programs seeking to divert offenders from penal incarceration and releasing those already institutionalized, to recognize that these efforts have been powerfully influenced by cost concerns and that these concerns have frequently overborne competing considerations of rehabilitation and human welfare.[94] The point, of course, is not that a penal system can or ought to ignore inevitable fiscal limitations. It is rather that from the beginning of its modern history the rehabilitative ideal has regularly proved itself incapable of defending its nature and integrity from the erosions of fiscal policy.

Even a brief consideration of the relevant history confirms the persistent tendency toward the debasement of the rehabilitative ideal in practical application. Indeed the evidence may justify the assertion sometimes made that rehabilitative theories of penal treatment have never been accorded a fair trial. That such is true today may appear supported by estimates that no more than five cents of every dollar currently spent on penal corrections are allocated to purposes that can be considered even remotely rehabilitative.[95] Yet there are countervailing arguments. Can it reasonably be assumed that in the great variety of social and political circumstances of the past two centuries in which rehabilitation has been attempted, none provided an environment favorable to fair testing? And if so, what reason is there for supposing that the nature of Western society will alter so as to provide more favorable circumstances in the next two hundred years—at least if techniques of rehabilitation threatening to basic political values are avoided?

A consideration of the phenomena of debasement leads naturally to the third and final proposition in the critique of the rehabilitative ideal. The proposition is that there is no evidence that an effective rehabilitative technique exists, that we do not know how to prevent criminal recidivism through rehabilitative effort. The statement of the proposition that has received widest attention was that of Robert Martinson. "With few isolated exceptions," he wrote in 1974, "the rehabilitative efforts that have been reported so far have had no appreciable effect on recidivism."[96] It can be said without derogatory intent that in many respects the statement is more interesting in its history than its content. For although the evaluation of rehabilitative research conducted by Martinson and his colleagues was no doubt more extensive than studies undertaken earlier, there was, in fact, little new about the skepticism expressed in the Martinson study of the rehabilitative capabilities of correctional programs or the existence of validated knowledge relevant to the avoidance of criminal recidivism. At least since World War II expressions of such skepticism have abounded in penological literature, as have criticisms of correctional entrepreneurs whose claims of significant reformative achievements were unsupported by scientific demonstration.[97] There is little to indicate, however, that public attitudes toward correctional policy were greatly affected by the earlier doubts and protest. One of the most important aspects of the Martinson study may well be that its immediate and widespread impact constitutes a demonstration of public attitudes in the 1970s receptive to the conclusions stated.

In a remarkably short time a new orthodoxy has been established asserting that rehabilitative objectives are largely unattainable and that rehabilitative programs and research are dubious or misdirected. The new attitudes resemble in

their dominance and pervasiveness those of the old orthodoxy, prevailing only a few years ago, that mandated rehabilitative efforts and exuded optimism about rehabilitative
capabilities.[98] Those who resist the hegemony of the new orthodoxy have challenged the criteria of success imposed by
the critics on rehabilitative programs and research and have
argued that the critics' own studies provide basis for at least
moderate optimism about future prospects of rehabilitative
attempts.[99] Some have suggested that the methods employed
in the modern attack on the rehabilitative ideal are often
more polemic and ideological in their nature than scientific.[100] Even though these controversies continue, it is not
too soon for certain general observations to be made. Proponents of rehabilitative research have argued with considerable force that to the extent the modern critique of the
rehabilitative ideal rests on scientific ignorance of many matters vital to rehabilitative programs, the indicated response is
not the abandonment of those efforts but, rather, the production of new knowledge.[101] Yet the proponents share with the
critics a profound dissatisfaction with most past examples
of rehabilitative research and practice. They express an
awareness of the complexities inherent in such endeavors that
was typically lacking in the enthusiasm for penal rehabilitation even in the recent past. A new spirit of caution pervades
claims about the rehabilitative potential of correctional programs; and the era when penal rehabilitationism can be accepted as the dominant mode of crime control seems more remote today than at many times in the past.

The several elements of the modern case against the
rehabilitative ideal are likely to be seen as of varying persuasiveness and cogency. Yet however persuasive the critique
significant questions remain. What attributes are likely to be
displayed by a penal policy in which traditional rehabilitative
aspirations have been eliminated or weakened? To what ex-

tent are the criticisms of penal rehabilitationism also applicable to alternative penal policies, and what additional problems may be anticipated from such policies? What future may reasonably be anticipated for the rehabilitative ideal in the closing decades of the twentieth century? These and related questions must now be considered.

T H R E E

What Future for
the Rehabilitative Ideal?

The last two decades of the twentieth century are not likely to bring full consensus on issues of crime and punishment. Nevertheless, one senses that in the modern decline of the rehabilitative ideal a notable turning point has been reached in American penal policy and, as in other periods of change, both perils and opportunities abound. The shift of perspective of American thought about crime and punishment does not of itself eliminate or even substantially alter the persistent and intractable obstacles to doing penal justice. In part this is true because the traditions and aspirations of the rehabilitative ideal are not dead; they still attract a large and powerful constituency. Much more to the point is the observation that the failures of American criminal justice in the last generation—its insensitivities, corruptions, and inefficiencies; the escalation of violence in American society; the losses in security of life, limb, and possessions—are failures of a system that as a whole cannot be regarded in any realistic sense as rehabilitative in purpose or effect. The contributions of the rehabilitative ideal to these failures have been at most peripheral.

Much of the attack on penal rehabilitationism ultimately voices broader concerns about the performance of the institutions of criminal justice. Operating a system of pains and penalties under any guise has proved a difficult and unsatisfactory business, and dissatisfactions become increasingly acute as the times encourage doubts and criticisms of governmental action of all sorts and at all levels. Many of the problems of penal rehabilitationism have their analogues in regimes embracing competing goals: just punishment, deterrence, and incapacitation. Thus conceptual difficulties with the notion of rehabilitation are matched by those encountered in efforts to define the concept of punishment proportional to the culpability of offenders. In all regimes, however oriented, the existence, guidance, and containment of discretion is a continuing concern, and in all of them, state power tends continually to impinge on political values. Determining the deterrent effects of differing levels of severity in penal sanctions poses problems for research at least as obdurate as those involved in tracing the impact of prison group-therapy programs on the recidivism of offenders. To complete the appraisal of the rehabilitative ideal, then, requires that attention be paid to problems inhering in alternative theories of penal treatment and that consideration be given to the contributions, if any, that the rehabilitative ideal may bring to American criminal justice in the future.

The meticulous delineation and analysis of policy options has not often characterized American political discourse during the past decade and a half. On the contrary, the political style has been largely one subjecting institutional performances to unremitting attack and articulating an impressive range of dissatisfactions and revulsions. Yet rational penal policy demands that the scrutiny of policy options proceed and that efforts be made to identify the problems characteristic of such alternatives and to inquire which of the old dilemmas are likely to persist.

In recent years, as was noted earlier, a number of groups with widely disparate motives and policy objectives united in an attack on the rehabilitative ideal.[1] One of the strange bedfellows is that group insisting on increasingly repressive measures in American law enforcement and penology. The extreme law-and-order advocates—the group described as adherents of the war theory of criminal justice—constitute one of the important and persistent realities of American political life and one of the principal limiting factors in American penal reform. Although the group rarely attempts coherent or comprehensive statements of position, and the individuals who compose it display great diversity of backgrounds and status, a few generalizations can be made. All of its members are deeply resentful of losses in the quality of American life caused by widespread criminality. Many reflect a kind of nostalgia for an earlier period of American society, real or imagined, when values were clear, the moral consensus was overwhelming, and in which the future was predictable and inviting.[2] Typically such persons believe that modern prisons are country clubs and that American judges are involved in an inexplicable conspiracy to subvert the public order by erecting obstacles to the detection and conviction of the guilty. Repressive regimes both in the prisons and on the streets prove attractive, not only because they are seen as solutions to the crime problem, but also because they express the values of discipline, vigor, and self-confidence largely lacking in contemporary American society.[3]

Programs of severe penal repression fail both in their ethical foundations and in their utility for practical policy making. Realism teaches one not to expect too much of the ethics of state action in any arena; but however minimal the expectations, the obligations of public morality entail more than imposing the same or greater brutalities on the criminal as those he has inflicted on his victim. The ethic of the war theory of criminal justice is one that conceives of the offender as an alien and in doing so induces a regression to primitive conceptions of penal justice. The offender is one outside the pale, and members of the in-group dealing with the peril to social interests that criminal behavior creates, are relieved of the ethical restraints governing the relations of human beings within society. The concept of "outlawry" in the ancient Germanic law still resonates in many modern attitudes and practices, and the morality that these attitudes advance is that of martial law.[4]

As a practical program of action the theories of extreme repression are unrealistic, even romantic in nature.[5] Proposals of extreme repression as deliberately adopted policy ignore certain salient features of contemporary American society. Prisons and prisoners today have political constituencies in a sense that was not true in midcentury. One of the consequences of the 1960s was a democratization of punishment. Thousands of middle-class citizens have had experiences in the recent past with arrest, conviction, and incarceration as a result of war protest, civil rights activities, and narcotics offenses. The concept of prisoner-as-alien has little appeal for these groups or for the many in sympathetic association with them.[6] Moreover, members of racial minorities, both in and out of prison, advance political interpretations of crime and punishment strongly antagonistic to policies founded on the war theory of criminal justice. Finally, the interventions of the courts and the judicial concept of prisoners' rights, however narrowly drawn, have proved radically inconsistent with penal regimes of the sort approved by extreme law-and-order advocacy.[7] To achieve the repression proposed by such advocates would involve a significant political transformation of American society, one demanding a much higher tolerance of punitive governmental interventions throughout society than at present exists. No one can say with assurance that such transformations will not occur in the future, but nothing in the present situation, despite the current vogue of capital punishment, suggests that a political consensus supportive of extreme penal repression will soon emerge.

Although a deliberate policy of extreme repression will al-

most certainly fail of general acceptance, the continuing advocacy of its objectives in the press and by public figures ex-
acerbates disharmony and social conflict. In addition, the
persistence of the war theory acts as a significant limitation
on other objectives of reform, whether those be rehabilitative,
humanitarian, the achievement of just punishment, or the
scaling down of the notoriously high levels of penal incarceration in the United States. The war theory, in short, stands
against efforts at compassionate penal reform or, for that
matter, any other penal theory seeking the consistent expression of a rational principle. Thus one may continue to see leg-
islatures directing the increased incarceration of offenders
while at the same time refusing to provide fiscal relief for the
consequent problems of institutional overcrowding.[8]

Nor do the prescriptions of radical criminology provide a
genuine alternative to the hegemony of the rehabilitative
ideal. Indeed, the dogma that the pathologies of criminal justice are the inevitable consequences of an unjust social order
is a counsel of despair, at least for those persons not yet ready
to man the barricades in an effort to overturn the corrupt and
decadent capitalist regime.[9] In short, the position is one that
largely abandons the effort at penal reform and amelioration
and seeks instead to overturn the structures of power and authority of an unjust social order.[10] It is far from clear that all
who advise this course oppose the concept of penal
rehabilitationism. The gist of the attack seems to be not that
the rehabilitative ideal attempts through coercive means to
impose societal values on offenders, but rather that the wrong
values are imposed; not that rehabilitationism is an instrument of social control, but that control is exercised by unjust
regimes. The examples of the Soviet Union and the People's
Republic of China suggest that conceptions of the extreme
malleability of human nature prevalent in socialist societies
make versions of the rehabilitative ideal congenial to such re-

gimes, however strongly elements of retribution and deterrence also figure in those systems.[11]

There is, however, another strand of thought which, although rejecting the revolutionary implications of radical
criminology, nevertheless associates crime with broader social
pathologies—unemployment, family dissolution, bad hous-
ing, and the like—and seeks the elimination or lessening of
crime by attacks on these conditions. There are probably few
persons of liberal political persuasion who do not share this
outlook to some degree. But appeals for general social reform
do not constitute a penal policy. Indeed, such advocacy of
broad social reconstruction may be employed by some as a
means to avoid thinking about or involvement in the hard
and disagreeable realities of crime and punishment. The advocacy of sweeping social changes primarily because they will
reduce crime is rarely sensible. Minimizing crime is a good,
but there are other social goals as important; and it is possible
that the objectives of crime control may often prove incompatible with other desired ends. Whether and to what extent
social reforms reduce the quantum of criminal behavior are
far from clear.[12] The system of criminal justice provides a
very narrow base from which to launch movements of fundamental social reconstruction, and one may reasonably doubt
the competence of criminologists, regardless of the disciplines
in which they have been trained, to achieve the brave new
world.[13]

It is apparent, then, that one must move to other areas if acceptable options to the hegemony of the rehabilitative ideal
are to be found. The weakening of penal rehabilitationism
marks a new era in thought about crime and punishment, but
it is an era that has as yet produced few theoretical innovations. Rather, the period is one in which old ideas about the
ends and means of criminal justice are being treated with a
new seriousness. Old concerns about deterring crime, the

matching of penalties to culpability, and achieving social defense through the incapacitation of potentially dangerous persons have been revived, and contentions rage over which of these goals should be admitted into a modern system of penal justice and which should be given dominant expression. Disputes surround the questions of whether and how far the decriminalization of conduct now punishable should proceed and the extent penal incarceration can and ought to be avoided in a modern system of penal sanctions. As yet, however, no new paradigm has emerged with the potency once displayed by the rehabilitative ideal to dominate thought, excite imagination, and impel social action. The modern eclecticism requires one concerned with contemporary movements of penal policy to identify strands of thought and to speculate how they might be incorporated into a larger synthesis.

One of the most interesting of such strands of thought, and perhaps one of the most important, is that expressed in modern doctrines of "just punishment" or "just deserts." The doctrines of just deserts generate formidable problems of definition. A comparatively full-blown version of the doctrine, however, is likely to include two principal assertions. First, the primary object of criminal sanctions is to punish culpable behavior. Although punishment may result in certain utilitarian benefits, notably the reduction of criminal behavior, the justification of punishment does not require such a showing; for it is moral and just that culpable behavior be punished.[14] Second, the severity of the sanctions visited on the offender should be proportioned to the degree of his culpability. The notion of desert both justifies the selection of the offender for penal treatment and also determines the severity of the penalty imposed on him.[15]

One of the most interesting questions that can be asked about the doctrine of just deserts is why the ideas it expresses are able to attract wide support in the last quarter of the twentieth century. The ideas are not new, but are, on the contrary, recurring themes in the history of penal thought. Retributive theories of punishment are among the most ancient, and the notion of penal proportion was central to the thought of reformers in the eighteenth-century Enlightenment, like Beccaria and Voltaire.[16] Yet upon reflection it becomes evident that the ideas of desert and penal proportion respond to some of the most basic concerns of modern men and women. The theories of just punishment strongly reaffirm the reality of moral values at a time when much in contemporary thought appears to challenge the conception of moral as well as legal responsibility; when the modern anarchy of values breeds feelings of loss and anomie; and when dwindling confidence in the future is obviously related to the erosion of the moral verities of the past.[17] Such considerations, however, explain the allegiance of only some of those who support theories of just deserts. For others the principal attractions are political in nature. Classical criminology, which arose in the eighteenth century and is closely related to some modern versions of just deserts doctrine, expressed a strong political awareness. It was formulated in large part to counter the capricious and irresponsible uses of state power that characterized Continental criminal procedure in the early modern period.[18] The same impulse to contain the powers of the state may be seen today in many contemporary supporters of the classical views. To achieve such containment, present-day adherents believe, penal sanctions must be definite and limited by law and must apply equally to all persons convicted in the criminal courts. Some of the policy implications of these views are clear: sentencing discretion is to be eliminated or sharply curtailed; the indeterminate sentence, that most characteristic product of penal rehabilitationism, must be abolished; no anticipation of social benefits can be permitted to justify any sentence that in its severity exceeds the deserts of the offender.[19]

The political dimensions and nuances of theories of just

deserts encompass more than sentencing and correctional practices, however; they extend to the problem of crime definition as well. The distinctive attribute of criminal behavior, in this view, is not only that it is dangerous to the interests of other individuals or the state, but rather that, in addition to the fact of harm, the behavior reveals an element of culpability. The principle of blameworthiness imposes restraint on the state by insisting on the relevance of facts and values that go beyond the interests and purposes of the political regime. Thus, the mens rea principle claims a small immunity from social exigencies by requiring the state to take into account the particular characteristics of the accused—his purposes, knowledge, and his mental and emotional capacities.[20] It is unlikely that any society has been saved from despotism by virtue of the mens rea doctrine, and indeed, oppressive regimes are adept at exploiting the doctrine for their own ends. Yet it is a significant fact that even totalitarian governments discern that to obtain legitimacy for their punitive measures they must on occasion demonstrate the criminal knowledge or purpose of the offender.[21]

Finally, in accounting for the attractions of the just deserts theories to many modern men and women, attention must be given to the strong egalitarian ingredient present in contemporary versions of the theories. There is no circumstance of American life in the past two decades more striking than the ascendancy of the value of equality in contemporary thought and political movements. It provides the assumptions for modern ethical theory and social activism.[22] It has strongly conditioned attitudes toward criminal justice: the contributions of the Warren Court to the constitutional law of criminal procedure, for example, were founded in large measure on convictions about the distorting effects of race and poverty on the penal process.[23] It underlies a large part of the current interest in white-collar crime. In such an environment the theories of just deserts are able to marshal strong support for their attack on the prevalence of sentencing disparities—sentencing practices that result in imposing penalties of widely varying severity on persons who commit similar offenses. Theories of just deserts, then, by advancing measures designed to limit the exercise of discretion within the system of criminal justice and by striking out at inequalities in institutional practices, reflect the values and aspirations of many people living in the late twentieth century.

A glance at the prior career of the blameworthiness principle is useful when speculating about the contributions that retributive theories may make to a new paradigm of criminal justice. Two features of the history are particularly striking. The first is that the notion of just deserts has survived, a fact of considerable interest when account is taken of the hostility with which the idea has often been greeted almost from the beginning of speculations about crime and punishment and its nearly complete neglect in the recent past.[24] The notion survives because it expresses a basic moral intuition: persons ought not to be subjected to the rigorous and stigmatic sanctions of the criminal law unless their conduct has merited it. There seems every reason to believe that this intuition will exert a continuing influence on the penal policy now emerging as it has, to a greater or lesser degree, on policies of the past.[25] The second observation, however, is that although the notion of just deserts has demonstrated great survival power, it has never wholly dominated the penal policy of any advanced society. On the contrary, it has been beset by competing concepts and interests, and its hold both on the theory and practice of criminal justice is never complete and is sometimes tenuous. In the modern world the just deserts notion must confront doubts about the moral autonomy of human beings, doubts engendered by powerful intellectual currents deriving from widely held assumptions about the nature of man and of human behavior. It must also withstand radical protests that criminal offenders are victims of a corrupt society and that the meting out of moral and legal condemnation on them by the agencies of such a society is bizarre and outrageous. The blameworthiness principle must compete with conceptions of penal deterrence and incapacitation. In many instances the preventive objectives of penal policy are so insistent that concerns about the shadings of offenders' moral culpability are seen as luxuries too expensive to indulge. It must also deal with the centrifugal forces of a pluralistic society which produce widely differing estimates within the community of the blameworthiness of behavior and the seriousness of the harms committed.[26] In short, the idea of just deserts has been part of a clamor of values and interests that policymakers in the past, with more or less deliberation and with varying success, have been required to accommodate and reconcile. The experience of the past suggests that the contributions of just deserts theory to a new consensus on penal policy, while likely to be significant, will again be limited by competing values.

A critique of the idea of just deserts, like that of the rehabilitative ideal, can best begin with its central concepts. Also as in the case of penal rehabilitationism, one immediately encounters conceptual difficulties. A primary source of these difficulties is in the underlying notion of commensurate penalties. It should be clear that practical expressions of the idea must always be highly approximate.[27] By what calculus or alchemy can the culpability of the offense be transformed into a criminal sanction? The difficulties of course are enhanced when the sentencing options available to the state for serious crimes are largely confined to varying terms of penal incarceration. Some advocates seeking to ease the problem have revived the talionic notion of "equivalent" penalties—an eye for an eye, a tooth for a tooth, a life for a life. The suggestion does little to relieve the difficulties. First, there are no equivalent penalties for many offenses defined in a modern criminal code.[28] What penalty can be regarded as equivalent to desecration of the flag? With reference to other sorts of crimes as well, the notion of equivalency is little more than a metaphor. The corporal punishment inflicted on a wife-beater is not the same as the offender's crime. To consider it so requires disregard of all subjective and many objective elements of loss.[29] Just as the notion of rehabilitation and the standards employed to determine whether or not it has occurred are matters largely of social definition and not of scientific demonstration, so also the concepts of desert and commensurate penalties defy precise formulation and application. This is far from saying that the notion of just deserts has no important contributions to make to penal policy. Indeed, what it has to offer is of vital consequence to any modern synthesis. The notion of just deserts performs the critical political function of locating the outer limits (and perhaps the minimum levels) of penal sanctions. It mandates a permissible range of penalties.

The legislative function of designating the outer limits of permissible penalties rarely lends itself to precision. The important consideration in this instance, however, is not precision, but is the perception that limits exist and that the principle of limitation is one that confines the penalty within a range defined by the concept of just deserts. Once this principle is conceded, the determination of the precise maximum levels poses exactly the sort of question that the processes of democratic lawmaking are designed to resolve. The theories of just deserts also contribute to the ordering of penalties. If one puts aside areas like abortion and the sumptuary offenses in which disputes rage over whether the conduct should be made criminal at all, it is likely that the notion of just deserts facilitates the classifying of offenses according to their relative seriousness.[30]

The doctrine of just deserts, then, makes important contributions to penal theory and practice by supplying principles for the necessary containment of state power within the system of criminal justice and for an acceptable ordering of penalties. Difficulties arise when more is demanded of the concept. Ideas of desert supply what Norval Morris calls limiting principles, not defining principles.[31] In this view of the matter, once desert has established the acceptable limits of punishment for the various crime categories (and the ranges may be relatively wide), a whole platoon of societal interests and values stands waiting to influence decisions concerning where, within those limits, penalties will be set in individual cases. The societal interests may be expressed in demands for the deterrence of criminal behavior or the incapacitation or rehabilitation of serious offenders. At the other extreme, social interest may be thought to require a maximum economy or parsimony of punishment: since punishment in itself is an evil, it may be argued, penalties less severe than those deserved should be imposed whenever such leniency is consistent with social interests.[32] The reflection and reconciliation of such social purposes in individual sentencing decisions, however, requires the exercise of judgment of officials possessed of some range of discretionary choice. It is at this point that serious controversy arises, for few contemporary attitudes are more evident than the suspicions and revulsions stimulated by the notion of official discretion. In consequence, the control and confinement of sentencing and correctional discretion are important attributes of nearly all modern policy proposals. In some, the resistance to sentencing discretion is adamant and uncompromising. The American Friends Service Committee, for example, insists: "Whatever sanction or short sentence is imposed is to be fixed by law. There is to be no discretion in setting sentences, no indeterminate sentences, and unsupervised street release is to replace parole."[33]

Sentencing disparities and inequities in the administration of parole have severely taxed the consciences of modern penal reformers, and properly so.[34] Unease about the widely varying sentences imposed on persons convicted of the same or similar offenses is not new, but the impetus to reduce such disparities has been dampened by the rehabilitative ideal. To the rehabilitationist, differences in penal treatment are not disparities so long as they reflect genuine therapeutic considerations: treatment is to be made commensurate with the criminal, not with his criminal act, and is to be distributed among offenders "according to their needs." When, however, confidence is lost in the rehabilitative capacities of penal programs and in the ability of parole boards and correctional officers to determine when reformation has been achieved, the rehabilitationist rationale for treatment differentials no longer serves, and the differences are seen as irrational and indefensible.

It would be wide of the mark to attribute all sentencing disparities to the influence of the rehabilitative ideal, but its waning has provided the occasion for modern proposals to eliminate such discrepancies. The suspicion arises that in moving to this worthy objective, some reformers have not fully calculated the costs of solutions that would substantially eliminate or radically truncate sentencing discretion. Ironically, limiting discretion in the interest of equality of treatment also limits the possibilities of justice in individual cases.[35] A just ordering of sanctions demands that account be taken of important variations in circumstances surrounding the commission of crimes as well as differences in the knowledge, purpose, and emotional states of the offenders. Some such differences are reflected in the statutory definitions of crimes, but no penal code, however thoughtfully articulated, can encompass all factors relevant to the varying deserts of offenders and hence to the ordering of their penalties. A statutory scheme that drastically inhibits the taking of these factors into account in the sentencing process therefore results in losses of justice and equity. Injustice may result from imposing different penalties on persons who commit the same or similar crimes, but as was recognized as early as Aristotle, injustice may also result from imposing the same penalty on those who commit significantly different crimes. The prevailing modern mood facilitates the perception of the first kind of injustice, but it may dampen concern for the second. These of course are questions of more or less; for perfect equity eludes all schemes. Yet one of the characteristic pathologies of some modern movements of penal reform appears to be a tendency toward those kinds of injustice that the late Mr. Justice Frankfurter identified (in a different context) as among the most serious: that is, "the enforced equality of unequals."[36]

The search for equality of treatment of those convicted of the same offense may also inhibit the realization of important social values and interests in the sentencing process. A recurring situation may illustrate the problem. Vandalism of property by young offenders is a continuing occurrence in virtually all communities. Many judges respond to the phenomenon by imposing penalties much lower than those authorized by statute. Destructiveness of this kind is seen as a phase of growing up, and dangers to the offender's self-image are perceived if he is labeled a serious criminal. With these considerations in mind, the court may accept informal arrangements of restitution as substitutes for fines or imprisonment; or if formal sanctions are employed, they may be set at the lowest levels. Occasionally, however, vandalism escalates into an epidemic. In such a situation the court may determine that to stem the tide of destruction, exemplary sentences must now be imposed. Accordingly, the next time such a case reaches the judge he imposes a jail term on the young offender and exacts a substantial fine. The convicted offender might be heard to complain: "But my friend who was before this court on the same charge six months ago was only admonished and sent home."[37] Assuming that the more severe sentence cannot be said to exceed the offender's just deserts when account is taken of the deliberateness of the behavior and the damage it has caused, one must ask, is the sentence nevertheless to be condemned solely because it is greater than those imposed earlier on persons who committed very similar acts? Some groups sponsoring sentencing reforms would argue so, even though the limits they would impose on sentencing discretion may involve considerable sacrifices of social advantage.[38] To deny the court authority to impose more severe penalties for the same or similar conduct when such measures are required to achieve deterrent or incapacitative ends may result in a general increase of severity of sentencing levels; for to ensure severity in cases where appropriate, the equality principle may mandate more severity than is required in other cases.

It is also important to be aware that the contribution of sentencing schemes to the achievement of genuine equality in the treatment of offenders within the system of criminal justice is highly limited, and that the effort to achieve equality by a relatively rigid sentencing structure may breed new inequalities of its own. Variations in police arrest policy toward young vandals—whether cases are adjusted at the precinct house or brought to court and vigorously prosecuted—will often have more to do with the differential impact of state power on offenders than vagaries in the exercise of sentencing power.[39] Moreover, perceptions that a sentencing structure is consistently sacrificing community interests by being either too lenient or too severe stimulate compensating adjustments within the system. A kind of hydraulic principle operates to enlarge the discretion of the police and prosecutors when it is denied to judges, and discretion in the former may be more erratic and difficult to contain than in the latter.[40]

It is no part of the purpose of this book to detail the essentials of a modern sentencing policy. This difficult and intricate task is today surely one of the most insistent objectives of penal reform. Several broad propositions can be stated, however. The concept of just deserts conceived as a principle for the containment of state power in the system of criminal justice is a first essential. Equality of treatment is a good, and within the limits of deserved punishment, differences in sentences of persons convicted of similar offenses can be justified only by affirmative showings of substantial social advantage. The control of discretion is more likely to be attained, not through efforts to extinguish it, but through the provision of guidelines for its exercise and through powers of scrutiny and revision in supervisory agencies.[41]

If in the search for alternatives to the rehabilitative ideal one moves from policies of just deserts to those dominated by considerations of deterrence or incapacitation and social defense, a set of common conclusions seems indicated. No one of these principles is sufficient in itself to determine all aspects of modern penal policy. Moreover, each of these principles must at some point be countered and contained by other principles. However compelling the requirements of deterrence and crime prevention may be, this society is not prepared to condone conviction and punishment of innocent persons, even if in doing so significant deterrent gains could be achieved.[42] One hopes also that reliance will not be placed on our highly fallible abilities to predict the future dangerousness of criminals in order to justify penalties going beyond the just deserts of the offender for the crime of which he is convicted.[43] Penal policy, then, gives every indication of retaining its pragmatic and eclectic character. For some critics this eclecticism is evidence of theoretical weakness; and it must be admitted that in recent decades the Western world has not lavished its theoretical virtuosity in areas of penal policy.[44] Nevertheless, the observation seems unduly harsh. The reality is that a wide variety of tasks are assigned to the system of criminal justice involving an impressive range of interests and purposes. The purposes and values involved are often in conflict, and the dissonance in theory reflects genuine incompatibilities. For the indefinite future a prime function of penal policy will be to reconcile interests and aspirations that are significantly inconsistent. The success of the necessary effort at reconciliation is doomed at the outset to be incomplete and disappointing, and such balance as is achieved is likely to prove unstable and temporary. Penal policy may camouflage and wise policy may minimize discord and futility in the administration of criminal justice, but they will not greatly alter the underlying social realities that give rise to the competing purposes and values.

What role is likely to be accorded the rehabilitative ideal in the emerging modern synthesis? One point seems clear: whatever functions are assigned to penal rehabilitationism in the remaining years of the twentieth century, they are likely to be peripheral rather than central to the administration of criminal justice. This is true not only because of the new awareness of the limited efficacy of rehabilitative programs and the other factors making up the modern critique of the rehabilitative ideal, but also because even an effective program of inmate reform contributes only tangentially to the strategy of public order. In that strategy the deterrence of the great majority of the population from serious criminal activity is always the consideration of first importance, not the rehabilitation or incapacitation of the much smaller number of persons convicted of criminal offenses. Moreover, in many crime categories the successful reform of offenders will not of itself reduce crime rates, except insofar as the incarceration and procedures associated with the rehabilitative effort produce an incidental deterrent effect.[45] Efforts to reform a murderer who has killed his wife in a domestic squabble will probably not reduce future homicides, in any event, because the wife-killer is not likely to recidivate. In crimes involving economic motivations, the reform of offenders will not prevent new recruits from entering similar criminal enterprises so long as opportunities for profit are perceived and the costs of criminal activity are not so high as to deter it.[46] There are other factors applicable particularly to incarcerative institutions that limit the role of penal rehabilitationism. The intervention of courts into prisons in the interest of the inmates' legal and constitutional rights tends to bureaucratize prisons, to standardize procedures and reduce the scope of the discretion in ways inconsistent with the individualization of treatment essential to a genuinely rehabilitative regime.[47] Indeed, the perception appears to be growing that such regimes are incompatible with the management of large penal institutions at minimal levels of order and efficiency because such regimes often weaken lines of administrative authority and open the door to inmate domination of institutional life with consequences of violence and terror for individual prisoners that are the very opposite of rehabilitative.[48]

Yet to recognize that the contributions of the rehabilitative ideal to modern penal policy are limited and peripheral is not to say that it has no valid contributions to make or that rehabilitative concerns will disappear in the decades ahead. On the contrary, for some purposes and with reference to certain groups, rehabilitative efforts constitute rational and morally valid responses to problems of penal treatment. Neither as individuals nor as a society are we able to escape the question of whether persons who come within our influence or control are better served by a posture of protective paternalism emphasizing educative and socializing influences or one that assumes the full moral autonomy and responsibility of such persons. The issue is inescapable because however distasteful to modern sensibilities the fact may be, neither posture is valid in all cases and each in varying degrees is appropriate in some cases. Moreover, no infallible calculus exists to distinguish the cases and to identify appropriate attitudes. It follows that oscillations may be anticipated in public policies relating to such matters as crime, welfare, child rearing, and education, in which now one and then the other

emphasis will be expressed. The principal danger of these oscillations arises when, by reason of enthusiasm or political
bias, we collectively forget the claims of alternative policies
and proceed rashly in disregard or ignorance of such claims.

There are influences of a more disturbing sort that also
militate against the sudden and total expiration of rehabilitative effort. The function of governmentally sponsored
and funded programs of rehabilitation in such areas as juvenile delinquency, addiction, mental health, and truancy is not
only to mitigate excruciating problems that produce community agitation and concern, but also to create the appearance
of doing so. Legislators are in constant need of "programs" to
demonstrate that "something is being done." Often what, if
anything, is to be done is far from clear. The remarkable facility of the rehabilitative ideal in supplying programs of the
mollifying sort has contributed to its survival in the past and
may, in spite of all that has occurred, continue to do so in the
future.

In what particular areas may rehabilitationism be expected
to make legitimate contributions to the administration of
criminal justice? Certain problems beset penal administration
regardless of its theoretical orientation; they must be faced
whatever role is ultimately accorded the rehabilitative ideal.
Even if the role is severely limited and the effort to make prisoners better and less dangerous is largely abandoned, penal
policy can hardly ignore the problem of prisoners being made
worse and more dangerous by the prison experience. There
appears to be a considerable division of sociological opinion
on whether or to what degree prisons are schools of crime.
Some findings suggest that the values encountered by most
offenders in prison are essentially the same as the those they
had already accepted before entering prison, and that the
prisons ought not to be regarded as significant sources of
new crime. However this may be, it must be clear that in many
particular cases the prison experience is devastating and trau-

matic.[49] Rupert Cross seems correct in the importance he accords to "what can best be described as 'anti-deformative action' in our prisons."[50] Considerations of both social policy and compassion urge that institutionally-related deterioration of prisoners be avoided whenever possible. Yet whatever is done, such anti-deformative efforts will almost certainly express many of the assumptions and much of the program of penal rehabilitationism. Rehabilitative technique and research, therefore, retain relevance for these problems.

If attention is directed to schemes of penal treatment administered outside of prison, a similar conclusion will be reached. Although contemporary trends are conflicting, there still exists a strong movement to avoid or minimize the use of incarceration for some offenders and to provide instead "community-based treatment." Such programs necessarily involve efforts to integrate offenders into the community and, at a minimum, to create employment and educational opportunities for them and perhaps to supply counseling and therapy.[51] Even if in some instances the dominant motive of such programs appears to be fiscal rather than rehabilitative, their nature results in a continuing demand for rehabilitative effort and personnel.

If it be assumed, as realism requires, that despite movements to minimize penal incarceration, prisons will continue to play a dominant role in American corrections for the balance of the century, certain questions of great importance arise.[52] What contributions in the past has the rehabilitative ideal made to the decency of prison regimes, and what losses in this respect may be expected to result from the decline of rehabilitationism? The questions are important because in the artificial conditions of prison life, minimum standards of personal security, health, and humane treatment are often breached, and gross violations of such standards occur with distressing regularity.[53] It is a historical fact that the great reforms in the physical and moral conditions of institutional life

have been accomplished largely by persons whose humanitarian impulses were joined with rehabilitative aspirations.[54]
Nor is this surprising. One revolted by the human consequences of cruelty and neglect in the prisons is not likely to be
insensitive to the disabilities suffered by prisoners because of
their own ignorance and habits of life, or less moved to remedy defects of character than those of the physical environment. Moreover, it will often be the case that the objectives
both of fundamental decency in the prisons and the rehabilitation of prisoners will appear to require the same measures.
In many penal institutions rehabilitative personnel have often
acted to moderate the harshness of prison life on individual
prisoners, to bring to the attention of the prison administration abuses and inefficiencies as they arise, to complain of
bad food and poor medical care, and on occasion to expose
intolerable conditions to the public.[55] The sober questions
arise, who will perform these moderating functions, where
will the impetus toward humane treatment come from, when
such personnel are eliminated or drastically reduced in numbers?[56] Experience has shown that public scrutiny is not
sufficient to obtain these ends. Prisons are out of sight and
out of mind. There is even reason to suspect that the public
generally resists knowledge of prison abuses.[57] At frequent
intervals throughout this century the press has disclosed the
recurrence of serious, even shocking, penal conditions. Each
revelation is greeted with incredulity and indignation, and
soon with amnesia. Rather than permitting these problems to
burden our individual consciences, we as a society have
tended to delegate the achievement of minimum decency in
the prisons to elite groups. In the past these groups were
made up of reformers motivated by religious zeal and humanitarian objectives.[58] Later, therapists and rehabilitationists performed a somewhat similar role. Today the task in
large part has been given over to federal judges. Under the
banner of the Fourteenth Amendment and civil rights legisla-

tion, judicial interventions into the prisons are taking place, and in many situations inequities and arbitrariness in the management of prisoners have been reduced and the physical conditions of jail and prison life improved. Although attended by genuine difficulties for prison administrators, the new judicial activism in the area of prisoners' rights has resulted in benefits that should be preserved and even extended. Nevertheless, so complete a reliance on judges is unwise. Judicial interventions are by their nature episodic. Sometimes the courts have shown surprising reluctance to remedy deplorable conditions, and often those initiating such litigation find their cases dismissed without decisions on the merits.[59] Moreover, the effectiveness of judicial scrutiny would be importantly enhanced if supported by an alert public opinion, or if that is too much to contemplate, by a rather larger group of educated and influential persons than has typically concerned itself with such problems in the past. In short, a division of ethical labor that allocates concerns about basic decency in the prisons to judges and relieves the rest of the community from responsibility is inadequate to our needs.

The relations of rehabilitationism to the decency of penal programs deserve another word. Despite what has just been said, some observers deny that on balance the rehabilitative ideal has contributed to the humanity of criminal justice.[60] One of the reasons is that the vocabulary of rehabilitation is often employed in penal institutions to surround and obscure with a cloud of euphemisms and misrepresentations the harsh realities prevailing there. In consequence, the true situations are hidden or distorted, and the task of rational reform is rendered more difficult or impossible. That there is at least some historical warrant for such complaints can hardly be denied. Yet the question arises whether this result, as well as many of the other charges levied against the rehabilitative ideal, stems from the presence of rehabilitative programs in

penal institutions or from the way in which the role of rehabilitation has been defined in the administration of penal
justice. So long as the success of prison programs is measured
by the degree to which reformation has been achieved, there
will be strong pressures on the institutions to exaggerate such
achievements and to present distorted descriptions of their
programs and problems. There are, however, alternative
definitions of the role. During the course of the decade just
past a strong current of opinion has arisen calling for voluntarism in the administration of institutional programs of education and rehabilitation.[61] Such programs are to be provided, but participation in them is to be at the option of the
inmates. Most important of all, the duration of the prisoner's
incarceration is to be determined without reference to
whether or not he elects to participate in such programs, and
his release is not to be conditioned on a finding that he has
been rehabilitated during his prison stay. On the contrary,
the prisoner should know his release date when he begins
service of his sentence or shortly thereafter. The rehabilitative programs supplied inmates, again to use the language
of Norval Morris, are to be facilitative rather than coercive
in nature.[62]

A strategy that would avoid conditioning prison release on
inmate participation in rehabilitative programs and upon
official determinations that an acceptable level of rehabilitation has been reached, may be defended, first, as that most
likely to achieve rehabilitative gains. Coercive strategies induce motives in both the prisoners and correctional personnel that inhibit or prevent inmate change. Under coercive regimes the goal of rehabilitation is imposed by the system; it is
rarely one originated or accepted by the prisoner. His objective is early release, and when release is accelerated by appearances of rehabilitation, the prisoner will studiously con-
coct such appearances.[63] For its part the correctional system is
asked to make judgments about the progress of the inmate to-

ward rehabilitation largely on the basis of his institutional behavior. Yet behavior in prison has little utility in predicting the behavior of prisoners after release.[64] Inevitably when parole decisions are found to be incapable of performing their intended function—the identification of prisoners ready for release—they will be employed to achieve other ends. The other purposes include the use of parole decisions as a device to reinforce institutional discipline. There is reason to hope that programs that facilitate a prisoner's own goals of education and self-improvement and are freed from the distorting effects of traditional regimes, will improve the efficacy of such programs.[65]

Yet assurances cannot now be made that facilitative regimes will produce widespread rehabilitative gains or substantially reduce criminal recidivism. In large part, justification must be made on other grounds. The question is not (or is not exclusively) whether facilitative strategies work, if by working is meant contributing significantly to crime control.[66] On the contrary, the central justification rests on a proposition of public morality. In dealing even with those who have seriously breached community norms of conduct, it is wrong for the state to strip all hope and opportunity for self-development from the human beings within its custody and care; it is accordingly part of the state's obligation to facilitate, where feasible, prisoners' aspirations for knowledge and growth.[67]

That the proposition will be given adequate practical expression in the years ahead is far from clear. Objections will be raised that programs contributing little to custodial administration and only marginally to crime control had best be avoided in the prisons. The educational and welfare needs of prisoners are only a small part of larger needs for such services. Indeed, it may be said, the case for large concerns and expenditures in behalf of those who have never been or have not yet become dangerous to the community is patently stronger than that for prisoners who have clearly identified themselves as community dangers or nuisances. In short, one may anticipate the modern emergence of the old principle of "least eligibility."[68] Closely related are the possible attitudes of legislators. It seems likely that in their search for programs to demonstrate concern for community anxieties, some legislators will be less drawn to proposals concerned with implementing minimum standards of ethical behavior toward prisoners than those promising prodigies of crime control. One hopes that such attitudes will not totally prevail, for special measures and strategies are demanded to counter the peculiar dangers that arise when, as in the prisons, the state intervenes massively in the lives and volition of persons. One of the promising prophylactic strategies is that which recognizes a state obligation to facilitate the self-development of inmates.

EPILOGUE

Considering the social requirements to which penal policy must in various ways respond, one concludes that the rehabilitative ideal will continue to influence the administration of criminal justice. Roles for rehabilitative effort must be conceded as long as we are concerned with efforts at de-carceration, avoiding the avoidable deterioration of human beings in penal confinement, and in maintaining defensible standards for the governance of those held in state custody.[1] This being true, there is a continuing need for the gathering of new knowledge concerning the efficacy of official efforts to accomplish such ends.[2] Experience with work-release programs, for example, has not been uniformly favorable. Nevertheless, success for some such programs has been claimed.[3] What generalizations can be made about the factors resulting in the success or failure of the undertakings, and what impacts on the participants can be reasonably anticipated? There is danger that new orthodoxies about the means and ends of penal administration may discourage inquiry into such questions and dry up research funds for those disposed to inquire.

Although there seems to be no prospect of the total banishment of the rehabilitative ideal from the theory and practice of criminal justice, attitudes toward it are likely to be wary in the closing years of this century. A statement made by Lionel Trilling over a generation ago still possesses acute relevance to the present: "Some paradox of our nature leads us, when once we have made our fellow men the object of our enlightened interest, to go on to make them the objects of our pity, then our wisdom, ultimately our coercion."[4] That alternative theories of penal justice—retributive, deterrent, those of social defense—likewise contain potentialities for debasement and serious abuse, does not invalidate the concerns and caution stimulated by penal rehabilitationism. Given the history through which American society has recently passed, it is hardly possible that the total benevolence of governmental interventions into persons' lives will be unthinkingly assumed or that the axiom of the identity of the interests of individuals and the state can soon again provide the assumptions for social action. It is just as well. For modern citizens of the world have learned that the interests of individuals and society are frequently adverse and that the assumption of their identity supplies the predicate for despotism.[5]

Wariness of the state and suspicion of authority in all of its various forms may be said to be the wisdom of many persons inhabiting the late twentieth-century world. It is, in part, a legitimate wisdom. Individuals and societies find it difficult, however, to distinguish an age's wisdom from its pathology, often because wisdom and pathology are the obverse sides of the same coin. Modern attitudes toward the exercise of official discretion, both within and outside the system of criminal justice, illustrate the fact. No one would be likely to deny that great and disturbing abuses of discretionary power have occurred in American society. It is also true that the problems of such abuse are particularly acute given the factors that produce interdependency in modern society and the complexities that make responsibility for abuse difficult to detect and establish. It therefore follows that procedures and devices to contain and challenge discretion must of necessity be an important modern preoccupation. Yet the preoccupation becomes pathological when it nourishes the belief that discretion can be avoided or when it prompts opposition to the programs and policies of social institutions solely because they rest in some measure on discretionary exercises of authority. The consequences of such attitudes are often harmful. One of these is that discretion is not eliminated but simply transferred from one agency or level to another; and the ones to whom the transfers are made may be less trustworthy receptacles of power and less easy to control than those from whom discretion was stripped. Another consequence is that the community may be incapacitated from doing what needs to be done and what its members desire to have done; for what needs to be done may unavoidably entail the exercise of discretion by public functionaries.

Much in modern attitudes toward authority reflects less a staunch individualism standing against the coercions and manipulations of the state than a decline of confidence in public purposes. The decline may result from despair about the capacity of individuals or private groups to influence the course of events, from self-indulgence raised to the level of a moral imperative, or other reasons. Sooner or later, however, this society must come to terms with social authority. Although the notion of there being an identity of social and individual interests is a chimera, there are social purposes which, if realized, contribute to a fuller humanity and are indeed the conditions for the achievement of human potentialities. Thus protection of persons and property from unwarranted aggressions by other members of the community must be accomplished at some level of adequacy, as must the relief of poverty and the care and protection of children, the mentally disadvantaged, and other members of the large and varied group of those unable to care for themselves.[6] Theories of rights which, if implemented, prevent or seriously obstruct the achievement of such social purposes are not likely to survive and contain the danger of breeding revulsions that strip public support from proper efforts to protect individuals from tyrannical governmental interventions. If a theory of rights prevents the achievement of social purposes, there is something amiss either in the theory of rights or in the conception of public purposes. Penal policy is concerned with achieving social purposes in a fashion that nevertheless protects the essential humanity of those who, for reasons of social defense, are placed in positions of extreme dependency. But in this era we all exist in a state of dependency, and how well we meet the problems of penal justice may foretell the degree of our success in dealing with matters of wider social concern.

Notes

Chapter 1

1. "What dramatically distinguished nineteenth century law from its eighteenth century counterpart was the extent to which the common law judges came to play a central role in directing the course of social change. Especially during the period before the Civil War, common law performed at least as great a role as legislation in underwriting and channeling economic development." M. HORWITZ, THE TRANSFORMATION OF AMERICAN LAW, 1780–1860 (Cambridge: Harvard University Press, 1977) 1; also at 80, 255–56. *Cf.* Bridwell, *Theme and Reality in American Legal History*, 53 IND. L. J. 449 (1978).

2. Letter of March 22, 1908. J. PEABODY, ed., THE HOLMES-EINSTEIN LETTERS (New York: St. Martin's Press, 1964) 37.

3. F. ALLEN, LAW, INTELLECT, AND EDUCATION (Ann Arbor: University of Michigan Press, 1979) 93 *et seq.* and *The Law as a Path to the World*, 77 MICH. L. REV. 157 (1978).

4. F. ALLEN, THE BORDERLAND OF CRIMINAL JUSTICE (Chicago: University of Chicago Press, 1964) 26. Compare the recent definitional statement in Schwitzgebel, *Development and Legal Regulation of Coercive Behavior Modification Techniques with Offenders*, National Institute of Mental Health, No. 2067 (Washington, D.C.: U.S. Govt. Printing Office, 1971): "Treatment is directed toward producing an enduring change in the behavior of an individual as he lives under natural conditions in the community. Included within the concept of treatment is an idea of restoration or improvement rather than restriction or disablement."

5. One of the most interesting accommodations of a dogma of crime causation to the assumptions of penal rehabilitationism involved the phrenology movement in 19th-century America. In the 1840s phrenology began to be applied in the New York prison system. W. LEWIS, FROM NEWGATE TO DANNEMORA (Ithaca, N.Y.: Cornell University Press, 1965) 236–37. "But if science 'proved' that the Creator had made some men moral and others irresponsible, the safety of society obviously required that criminals be given proper treatment. People with peaked heads or with bumps behind their ears should not be placed in positions of responsibility or temptation. The most extreme cases should be carefully isolated in special hospitals, where improvement under the guidance of trained phrenologists was certain to secure public safety." D. DAVIS, HOMICIDE IN AMERICAN FICTION, 1798–1860 (Ithaca, N.Y.: Cornell University Press, 1957) 25–26.

6. There is abundant historical documentation. See especially G. DE
   BEAUMONT AND A. DE TOCQUEVILLE, ON THE PENITENTIARY SYSTEM IN
   THE UNITED STATES AND ITS APPLICATION IN FRANCE (Carbondale, Ill.:
   Southern Illinois University Press, 1964). On the treadmill, see D.
   SCHNEIDER, THE HISTORY OF PUBLIC WELFARE IN NEW YORK STATE,
   1609–1866 (Chicago: University of Chicago Press, 1938) 152–55.

7. J. HOWARD, THE STATE OF THE PRISONS IN ENGLAND AND WALES (4th
   ed.) (London, 1792). A useful summary of his career may be found in
   D. HOWARD, JOHN HOWARD (New York: Archer House, 1958).

8. Proverbs 13:24. See also Proverbs: 19:18.

9. Malachi 3:2–3; Job: 5:17–18. And see 1 Corinthians 11:32; Hebrews
   12:5–11; Revelations 3:19.

10. *The Clouds* 1409–19.

11. NICOMACHEAN ETHICS 2. 3. 1104b. From an early date the medical anal-
    ogy is frequently employed in the literature of rehabilitation. Thus
    Plato writes, "The best kind of purification is painful, like similar cures
    in medicine." LAWS 5. 735–36. Thomas Aquinas: "just as the physician
    of the body restores the sick man to health, if possible, without cutting
    off a limb, but if this is unavoidable, cuts off the limb which is least indis-
    pensable, in order to preserve the life of the whole body, so too he who
    desires his brother's amendment should, if possible, so amend him as
    regards his conscience that he keeps his good name." SUMMA
    THEOLOGICA 2–2. Q 33, A 7. References to prisons as "moral hospitals"
    abound in the American nineteenth-century writing. See quotations in
    S. J. SANSWEET, THE PUNISHMENT CURE (New York: Mason and Char-
    ter, 1975) 141; W. LEWIS, *supra* note 5 at 252.

12. LAWS 9, 10.

13. THE CITY OF GOD 19. 16.

14. SUMMA THEOLOGICA 2–2. Q 33, A 1.

15. There is an extensive historical literature. One useful survey is M.
    GRUNHUT, PENAL REFORM (Oxford: Clarendon Press, 1948).

16. B. WOOTEN, SOCIAL SCIENCE AND SOCIAL PATHOLOGY (London: George
    Allen and Unwin, 1959) 210–21; C. LASCH, HAVEN IN A HEARTLESS
    WORLD (New York: Basic Books, 1977) 100–02. P. ROAZEN, FREUD: PO-
    LITICAL AND SOCIAL THOUGHT (New York: Vintage Books, 1968)
    290–91.

17. 337 U.S. 241, 247–48 (1949).

18. F. ALLEN, THE CRIMES OF POLITICS (Cambridge: Harvard University
    Press, 1974) 4–5.

19. *Id* at 6–7.

20. F. ALLEN, *supra* note 4, at 31–32.

21. STRUGGLE FOR JUSTICE (New York: American Friends Service
    Committee, 1971) 83. An earlier somewhat similar statement was made

in H. PACKER, THE LIMITS OF THE CRIMINAL SANCTION (Stanford, Calif.: Stanford University Press, 1968) 12–13.

22. Holder v. Superior Court, 269 Cal. App. 2d 314, 74 Cal. Rptr. 853, 855 (1969).

23. DEERING'S CALIFORNIA CODE ANN. § 1170(a)(1) (1977). The section continues as follows: "The Legislature further finds and declares that the elimination of disparity and the provision of uniformity of sentences can best be achieved by determinate sentences fixed by statute in proportion to the seriousness of the offense as determined by the Legislature to be imposed by the court with specified discretion."

24. Rubin, *New Sentencing Proposals and Laws in the 1970's*, 43 FED. PROB. 3 (June 1979); Skrivseth, *Abolishing Parole: Assuring Fairness and Certainty in Sentencing*, 7 HOFSTRA L. REV. 281 (1979); Glick, *Mandatory Sentencing: The Politics of the New Criminal Justice*, 43 FED. PROB. 3 (March 1979); Zalman, *The Rise and Fall of the Indeterminate Sentence*, 24 WAYNE L. REV. 857 (1978). As to good time credit, note the reduction of such allowances effected in Michigan by popular initiative. MCL § 800.33 (1978). A proposed revision of the federal statutes would also reduce good time credit. S. 1437, 95th Cong. 2d Sess. § 3824(b) (1978). But observe the opposite tendency in ILL. REV. STAT. chap. 38, §§ 1003–3–3, 1003–6–3.

25. See REPORT OF THE GOVERNOR'S PANEL OF JUVENILE VIOLENCE (Albany, 1976). In 1976 the New York Legislature enlarged periods of custodial confinement for juveniles committing "designated felonies" by an amendment to the Family Court Act. McKINNEY'S CONS. LAWS OF NEW YORK § 753a. In 1978 the age of criminal capacity of children was lowered, in some instances to 13, for specified felonies. Such children are, at least initially, to be processed in the criminal courts rather than the Family Court. McKINNEY'S CONS. LAWS OF NEW YORK (Penal Law) § 30.00. These innovations evoked adverse editorial comments in the N.Y. TIMES: *Going Too Far on Juvenile Crime* (January 27, 1979); *More Effective Juvenile Justice* (May 29, 1979).

26. It is said that between the decision of Furman v. Georgia, 408 U.S. 238 in 1973, and August 1, 1977, thirty-four American States enacted new death-penalty laws. H. KERPER, INTRODUCTION TO THE CRIMINAL JUSTICE SYSTEM (J. Israel, 2d ed.) (St. Paul, Minn.: West Publishing Co., 1979) 337.

27. Allen, *Central Problems of American Criminal Justice*, 75 MICH. L. REV. 813 (1977). The periods of agitation began early in American history. Thus a member of a New York legislative commission is quoted as saying in 1822: "Our newspapers teem with relations of crime of every dye. Our cities, villages, and manufactories are frequently in flames. . . . It is understood that connected bands of horse stealers and counterfeiters extend from Canada, through several points of the Union. The mails of

the United States no longer afford security. Felonies that affect the stability of our monied institutions are becoming common." W. Lewis, *supra* note 5, at 64–65.

28. Certain of these themes were sounded in the well-known report of the American Friends Service Committee, *supra* note 21. See also Becker and Horowitz, *Radical Politics and Sociological Research: Observations on Methodology and Ideology*, 78 Am. J. Soc. 48 (1972); Platt, *Prospects for a Radical Criminology in the United States*, 5 Crime and Social Justice 2 (Fall–Winter 1974); Platt and Takagi, *Intellectuals for Law and Order: A Critique of the Realists*, 8 *id.* 1 (Fall–Winter 1977).

29. The American Friends Service Committee's report, *supra* note 21, was also influential in promoting these positions. They are articulated with varying emphases in most of the literature on correctional and sentencing reform in the 1970s. Perhaps the most unqualified expressions are those found in A. von Hirsch, Doing Justice (New York: Hill and Wang, 1976).

30. Two works that received considerable attention in the 1970s are illustrative: E. van den Haag, Punishing Criminals (New York: Basic Books, 1975); J. Wilson, Thinking about Crime (New York: Vintage Books, 1977).

31. F. Allen, *supra* note 18, at 72–77.

32. A. Platt, The Child Savers (Chicago: University of Chicago Press, 1969, 1977).

33. There is an extensive literature on these matters. Basic to any study is G. de Beaumont and A. de Tocqueville, *supra* note 6, which first appeared in Paris and Philadelphia in 1833. Among the large number of other useful accounts, see: H. E. Barnes, The Evolution of Penology in Pennsylvania (Indianapolis: Bobbs-Merrill, 1927); D. Dix, Remarks on Prisons and Prison Discipline in the United States (Philadelphia, 1845); W. Lewis, *supra* note 5; D. Rothman, The Discovery of the Asylum (Boston: Little, Brown, 1971): D. Schneider, *supra* note 6; N. K. Teeters and J. D. Shearer, The Prison at Philadelphia: Cherry Hill, The Separate System of Prison Discipline, 1829–1913 (New York: Columbia University Press, 1957).

34. Assertions of the uniqueness of the American antebellum experience advanced in D. Rothman, *supra* note 33, are ably criticized in Schneider, *The Rise of Prisons and the Origins of the Rehabilitative Ideal*, 77 Mich. L. Rev. 707 (1979). See also S. Schlossman, Love and the American Delinquent (Chicago: Chicago University Press, 1977) 36, "It is impossible to understand the genesis of American juvenile corrections—its goals, institutional formats, and pedagogical techniques—without reference to the trans-Atlantic context of early nineteenth-century penal and educational reform." For many, the evidence relating to English experience in the late 18th and early 19th cen-

tury recently amassed in M. IGNATIEFF, A JUST MEASURE OF PAIN (New York: Pantheon Books, 1978), requires further modification of assumptions concerning the uniqueness or priority of American reforms.

35. G. DE BEAUMONT AND A. DE TOCQUEVILLE, *supra* note 6.

36. "Before 1775, imprisonment was rarely used as a punishment for felony. At the Old Bailey . . . imprisonments accounted for no more than 2.3 percent of the judges' sentences in the years between 1770 and 1774." M. IGNATIEFF, *supra* note 34, at 15. See also J. HOWARD, *supra* note 7, at 19; M. FOUCAULT, DISCIPLINE AND PUNISH (New York: Pantheon Books, 1977) 117, 234; W. D. LEWIS, *supra* note 5, at 7; D. M. SCHNEIDER, *supra* note 6, at 141–42.

37. Hobbes reveals familiarity with uses of imprisonment for punishment in the 17th century. LEVIATHAN 2. 28. See also J. HOWARD, *supra* note 7, at 109; M. GRUNHUT, *supra* note 15, at 12; Langbein, *The Historical Origins of the Sanction of Imprisonment for Serious Crime*, 5 J. LEG. STUD. 35 (1976).

38. There are many accounts of these practices. See, *e.g.*, G. DE BEAUMONT AND A. DE TOCQUEVILLE, *supra* note 6, at 41, 83–84: and other works cited in note 33 *supra*.

39. See works cited in note 33 *supra*.

40. Lieber, *Translator's Preface* (1833) in G. DE BEAUMONT AND A. DE TOCQUEVILLE, *supra* note 6, at 6.

41. G. DE BEAUMONT AND A. DE TOCQUEVILLE, *supra* note 6, at 44, 136; D. ROTHMAN, *supra* note 33, at 213; D. SCHNEIDER, *supra* note 6, at 214–15, 318–19.

42. See works cited *supra* note 33.

43. Evidences of this current of thought in the popular literature of the times is presented in D. DAVIS, *supra* note 5, at 312–13. The view was frequently contested, however. D. SCHNEIDER, *supra* note 6, at 212–13.

44. Brisbane, *Social Destiny of Man: or, Association and Reorganization of Industry* (1840) in W. HUGGINS, ed., THE REFORM IMPULSE, 1825–1850 (New York: Harper and Row, 1972) 231.

45. Quoted in H. COMMAGER, THEODORE PARKER (Boston: Beacon Press, 1947) 171. On another occasion Parker is recorded as saying: "To change the treatment of criminals, we must change everything else." *Id.* at 175–76. See also D. DAVIS, *supra* note 5, at 11.

46. This fact was apparent to contemporary observers. Thus Alexis de Tocqueville wrote: "There is not a country in the world where man more confidently takes charge of the future, where he feels with more pride that he can fashion the universe to please himself. It is a movement of the mind which can only be compared with that which brought about the discovery of the New World three centuries ago." JOURNEY TO AMERICA (J. Mayer ed.) (New Haven: Yale University Press, 1959) 183.

Among other relevant materials are D. DAVIS, ed., ANTE-BELLUM REFORM (New York: Harper and Row, 1967); W. HUGGINS, *Introduction*, *supra* note 44, at 1 *et seq.*; C. GRIFFIN, THEIR BROTHERS' KEEPERS (New Brunswick, N.J.: Rutgers University Press, 1960); P. MILLER, THE LIFE OF THE MIND IN AMERICA (New York: Harcourt, Brace and World, 1965); R. WELTER, THE MIND OF AMERICA, 1820–1860 (New York: Columbia University Press, 1975).

47. 5 HARVARD CLASSICS (C. Eliot ed.) (New York: Collier and Son, 1909) 45.

48. Mann, *Twelfth Annual Report of the Board of Education, Together with the Twelfth Annual Report of the Secretary of the Board* (Boston, 1849) 54–60; A. DE TOCQUEVILLE, *supra* note 46, at 196.

49. C. GRIFFIN, *supra* note 46, at 7; P. MILLER, *supra* note 46, at 32–33.

50. M. HOROWITZ, *supra* note 1, passim. Professor Horowitz supplies a quotation from a legal writer in 1829 that may be seen as the analogue of the Emerson statement in the text: "At no time has there been such a spirit of improvement pervading the country, as at present. The vast plans, indeed, which are now in embryo in most of the States for *turnpikes, canals, railroads, bridges*, and other means to facilitate internal communication, are almost without number." *Id.* at 66.

51. Typical expressions may be found in A. DE TOCQUEVILLE, *supra* note 46, at 60–61, 72, 75, 268–69.

52. E. SHORTER, THE MAKING OF THE MODERN FAMILY (New York: Basic Books, 1975) 65.

53. Sexton v. Wheaton, 21 U.S. (8 Wheat.) 229, 239 (1823).

54. Varying statements of these propositions pervade the literature of the times. D. DAVIS, *supra* note 5, at 9, 140–41: W. HUGGINS, *supra* note 44, at 12–13; C. LASCH, *supra* note 16, at 169; D. ROTHMAN, *supra* note 33, at 220; A. DE TOCQUEVILLE, 1 DEMOCRACY IN AMERICA (New York: Vintage Books, 1954) 315; H. COMMAGER, *supra* note 45, at 175. Professor Schlossman finds that the family model did not strongly affect actual institutional practices until near midcentury. *Supra* note 34, at 32.

55. ILL. LAWS (1899), *Juvenile Courts* § 21, "This act shall be liberally construed, to the end that its purpose may be carried out, to-wit: That the care, custody and discipline of a child shall approximate as nearly as may be that which should be given by its parents."

56. The novelist, Charles Brockden Brown, observed: "From the miscarriage of a scheme of frantic innovation [the French Revolution], we conceive an unreasonable and undiscriminating dread of all change and reform." D. DAVIS, *supra* note 5, at 50. See also W. HUGGINS, *supra* note 44, at 19; D. ROTHMAN, *supra* note 33 passim; A. DE TOCQUEVILLE, *supra* note 46; at 95.

57. Weaver, *Introduction* to SHORTER NOVELS OF HERMAN MELVILLE (New York: Grosset and Dunlap, 1928) xxix, "Both men [Hawthorne and Melville] from their youth, had felt the flagrant and stubborn discord between the actual and the ideal, between fact and aspiration."

58. Tocqueville wrote in his journal: "Up to now we have met a great many people who have studied the matter much and are doubtful whether one could succeed in *reforming* criminals. . . . We have more and more reason to make the same comment." *Supra* note 46, at 205. But in their famous report on the American penitentiary system Beaumont and Tocqueville reach a less pessimistic view: "Yet if we consider all the means employed in the prisons of the United States, in order to obtain this complete regeneration of the wicked it is difficult to believe that it should not be sometimes the reward of so many efforts." *Supra* note 33, at 87: also *id*. 89–90. Discouragement about the prevalence of crime and skepticism or disbelief in the possibilities of rehabilitation were frequently expressed. See also M. FOUCAULT, *supra* note 36, at 264–65: W. LEWIS, *supra* note 5, at 91, 101–02, 191, 249–50; C. PEIRCE, CRIME: ITS CAUSES AND CURE (Boston, 1854).

59. "This principle is modified from time to time in the casual speech of educators, in the training programs available for selected students in the sciences, and in the treatment of a small number of prisoners, but it remains unique and is the most influential assumption about man in the contemporary Chinese view." D. MUNRO, THE CONCEPT OF MAN IN CONTEMPORARY CHINA (Ann Arbor: University of Michigan Press, 1977) 20; and see *id*. at 19, 63, 104.

60. *Id*. at 19 *et seq*., 104.

61. Professor Munro comments: "An understanding of the relative absence in China of belief in innate defects of natural endowment may help Americans to comprehend the extraordinary faith and optimism the Chinese place in the educational system for the solution of the most vital social issues of the day: Alter people's conduct with educational means and thereby solve the problem." *Id*. at viii; see also *id*. at 118–19, 154, 185. The importance of heroes or models may be a characteristic of societies in which a revolutionary tradition is still strong. Such was true of antebellum America. See also R. DE GEORGE, SOVIET ETHICS AND MORALITY (Ann Arbor: University of Michigan Press, 1969) 114–15: "The interests of a Soviet 'saint' would coincide with the interests and demands of society as enunciated by the Party; he would be a creative though obedient, selfless, dedicated communist. This is the ideal New Man of Soviet society. This is the man Soviet leaders are trying to produce."

62. Although descriptions in English of Chinese penal methods are not complete, the main outlines can be sketched with reasonable confidence. Descriptions in the text are based largely on the published

memoirs of former political prisoners of the Chinese regime. The first is A. AND A. RICKETT, PRISONERS OF LIBERATION (New York: Cameron Associate, 1957). The writers, a married couple and young graduate students who were studying in China when the present regime came to power, proved susceptible to the rehabilitative program, and upon release wrote a generally approving description of the procedures they observed. At the other extreme is H. RIGNEY, FOUR YEARS IN A RED HELL (Chicago: Henry Regnery, 1976). Father Rigney, a Catholic priest, persisted in his strong animosity to the People's Republic and to the penal program in the prisons. Third is BAO RUO-WANG (J. PASQUALINI) AND R. CHELMINSKI, PRISONER OF MAO (New York: Coward, McCann and Geoghegan, 1973). The principal author is the off-spring of a mixed European and Chinese marriage, who had never been out of China at the time of his imprisonment. While grudgingly conceding the partial effectiveness and merit of some features of the prison program, he is generally skeptical and sometimes hostile. It is striking that although the authors of these memoirs brought very different backgrounds and motivations to their prison experiences, the descriptions of the penal methods they observed are in substantial accord. The consistency of the accounts adds confidence in their reliability. In addition, a principal source of information is AMNESTY INTERNATIONAL, POLITICAL IMPRISONMENT IN THE PEOPLE'S REPUBLIC OF CHINA (London, 1978), which collects printed information from a wide variety of sources. Other materials are cited in the text where relevant.

63. The Act for Reform Through Labour, adopted by the Government Administration Council on August 26, 1954, states as its purposes, "To punish all counterrevolutionary and other criminal offenders and to compel them to reform themselves through labour and become new persons." AMNESTY INTERNATIONAL, *supra* note 62, at 74–76. Manifold instances of rehabilitative motivations revealed in practice may be found in the literature. BAO RUO-WANG AND R. CHELMINSKI, *supra* note 62, at 32–33, 514–55; A. AND A. RICKETT, *supra* note 62, at 118–19; Paragon, *The Administration of Justice in New China*, 83 CASE & COMMENT 42, 52 (November–December 1978).

64. Among the purposes stated in The Law for Reform Through Labour, *supra* note 63, is "to educate offenders about admitting their guilt." AMNESTY INTERNATIONAL, *supra* note 62, at 135. For other illustrations relating to the securing and uses of confessions see *id*. at 45–54; BAO RUO-WANG AND R. CHELMINSKI, *supra* note 62, at 73; A. AND A. RICKETT, *supra* note 62, at 201–02. The content of a confession introduced in a trial for homicide is revealed in a transcript published in the American press: "I committed this crime because I wasn't spending much time studying political thought, and I have a very low political and socialist consciousness. During the Cultural Revolution, I came under the influence of Lin Riao and the Gang of Four. I don't know what the law

is and I have bourgeois ideas. Because I could not achieve my personal aims, I did not consider the interests of the state or of other people, so I threw everything to the wind and did what I wanted. I never considered the serious consequences of my actions when I committed the crime." Chi and Chi, *Crime and Punishment in China*, N.Y. TIMES MAGAZINE 48 (October 7, 1979).

65. AMNESTY INTERNATIONAL, *supra* note 62, at 78, 137–39; A. AND A. RICKETT, *supra* note 62, at 121, 169–70, 172, 200; Hinkle and Wolff, *Communist Interrogation and Indoctrination of "Enemies of the State"*, 76 A.M.A. ARCH. NEUR. AND PSYC. 156 (1956). Techniques of group criticism have been employed extensively in other societies, both in and out of the prisons. They were a feature of the Oneida Community in nineteenth-century America. C. ROSENBERG, THE TRIAL OF THE ASSASSIN GUITEAU (Chicago: University of Chicago Press, 1968) 19–20.

66. Vivid accounts were given in BAO RUO-WANG AND R. CHELMINSKI, *supra* note 62, at 58–60, 81. See also H. RIGNEY, *supra* note 62, at 31–32.

67. "Compulsory labor is the main method of 'reforming' prisoners—the test whereby they will prove that they have reformed—whereas 'education' is used only as a complementary method." AMNESTY INTERNATIONAL, *supra* note 62, at 77. See also *id.* at 79; BAO RUO-WANG AND R. CHELMINSKI, *supra* note 62, at 86.

68. One of the most striking instances of indeterminacy is the imposition of a sentence of capital punishment with a two-year suspension of execution to observe the effects. AMNESTY INTERNATIONAL, *supra* note 62, at 63. See also *id.* at 79; BAO RUO-WANG AND R. CHELMINSKI, *supra* note 62, at 39–40, 99–199.

69. See *supra* note 61.

70. The number of executions in the immediate aftermath of the revolution has been estimated to be as high as 800,000. There is evidence of a large number of executions since the purge of The Gang of Four in late 1976. AMNESTY INTERNATIONAL, *supra* note 62, at 29, 63–65.

71. *Id.* at 13.

72. *Cf.* R. HEILBRONER, THE FUTURE AS HISTORY (New York: Harper Torch Books, 1968) 114.

73. *Review* in S. ORWELL AND I. ANGUS, 4 THE COLLECTED ESSAYS, JOURNALISM AND LETTERS OF GEORGE ORWELL (New York: Harcourt, Brace, Jovanovich, 1968) 91. See also E. GOFFMAN, ASYLUMS (New York: Doubleday, Anchor Books, 1961) 12.

74. See, *e.g.*, D. DAVIS, *supra* note 5, at 180; A. DE TOCQUEVILLE, *supra* note 46, at 255.

75. Wisconsin v. Yoder, 406 U.S. 205, 233 (1972). Compare the statement of Mr. Justice Blackmun in Planned Parenthood v. Danforth, 428 U.S. 52, 75 (1976), "Any interest the parent may have in the termination of

the minor daughter's pregnancy is no more weighty than the right of privacy of the competent minor mature enough to have become pregnant."

76. C. Lasch, *supra* note 16, at 13–15; C. Lasch, The Culture of Narcissism (New York: W. W. Norton, 1978) 154–55; S. Schlossman, *supra* note 34, at 71; E. Shorter, *supra* note 52, at 276–77.

77. C. Lasch, *supra* note 16, at 134: S. Schlossman, *supra* note 34, at 76.

78. C. Lasch, *supra* note 16, at 18.

79. These consequences have been noted in areas such as those involving rights against child abuse. Divoky, *Child Abuse: Mandate for Teacher Intervention?* Learning 4 (April 1976); Wald, *State Intervention on Behalf of "Neglected" Children: A Search for Realistic Standards*, 27 Stan. L. Rev. 985 (1975). See also Gaylin, *In the Beginning: Helpless and Dependent* in W. Gaylin, I. Glasser, S. Marcus, and D. Rothman, Doing Good: The Limits of Benevolence (New York: Pantheon Books, 1978) 32; I. Illich, Toward a History of Needs (New York: Pantheon Books, 1978) 43–44; C. Lasch, *supra* note 16, at 14, 91.

80. C. Lasch, *supra* note 16, 128–30; E. Shorter, *supra* note 52, at 270–71.

81. One of the more remarkable arguments for federal intervention in the area of TV advertising is that of a child psychiatrist: "Furthermore, the advertisements encourage confrontation and alienation on the part of children toward their parents and undermine parents' child rearing responsibilities." *Federal Trade Commission Staff Report on Television Advertising to Children* (February 1978) 103–04.

82. The literature is extensive. See, *e.g.*, D. Bell, The Cultural Contradictions of Capitalism (New York: Basic Books, 1976) 168; C. Lasch, *supra* note 16, at 118, 124–25; P. Reiff, The Triumph of the Therapeutic (London; Chatto and Windus, 1966) 219, 243; E. Shorter, *supra* note 52, 7–8, 254.

83. "No other institution seems to work so badly, to judge from the volume of abuse directed against it in a growing wish to experiment with other forms." C. Lasch, *supra* note 16, at 130.

84. Banner, *Religious Benevolence as Social Control: A Critique of an Interpretation*, 60 J. Am. Hist. 23 (1973) and see *supra* note 61.

85. C. Lasch, *supra* note 76, at 125.

86. "America's commitment to compulsory education of its young now reveals itself to be as futile as the pretended American commitment to compulsory democratization of the Vietnamese." I. Illich, Deschooling Society (New York: Perennial Library, 1972) 94–95. See also *id.* at 45–46; I. Illich, *supra* note 79, at 68–69; C. Jencks, Inequality (New York: Harper Colophon Books, 1972) 95, 255; C. Lasch, *supra* note 76, at 127–30.

87. I. ILLICH, *supra* note 86, at 159; C. LASCH, *supra* note 76, at 25–26.

88. The loss of confidence in American public education appears to have become pervasive in American society by the time the Coleman Report appeared. J. COLEMAN, EQUALITY OF EDUCATIONAL OPPORTUNITY (Washington, D.C.: U.S. Govt. Printing Office, 1966). There were many individual expressions of disillusionment or unease at much earlier date, however. E. CUBBERLEY, PUBLIC SCHOOL ADMINISTRATION (Boston: Houghton-Mifflin, 1916) 338; C. PEIRCE, *supra* note 58, at 23–24, 33; E. THORNDIKE, EDUCATION AS CAUSE AND SYMPTOM (New York: Macmillan, 1939) 69.

89. Mann, *The Great Equalizer of the Conditions of Men*, TWELFTH ANNUAL REPORT OF THE BOARD OF EDUCATION TOGETHER WITH THE TWELFTH ANNUAL REPORT OF THE SECRETARY OF THE BOARD (Boston, 1849), quoted in W. HUGGINS, *supra* note 44, at 141.

90. Fiske, *Controversy Is Growing Over Basic Academic Competency*, N.Y. TIMES (April 19, 1978); Golden, *Functional Tests Hit By Panel*, MIAMI HERALD (February 16, 1978).

91. C. JENCKS, *supra* note 86, at 7–11, 29, 53, 90, 109, 255–56. See also I. ILLICH, *supra* note 86, at 12. *Cf.* D. LEVINE AND M. BANE, eds., THE "INEQUALITY" CONTROVERSY: SCHOOLING AND DISTRIBUTIVE JUSTICE (New York: Basic Books, 1975).

92. C. JENCKS, *supra* note 86, at 16–17, 24.

93. *Id.* at 135.

94. H. LEVY AND D. MILLER, GOING TO JAIL: THE POLITICAL PRISONER (New York: Grove Press, 1971) 103.

95. F. ALLEN, *supra* note 18, at 8; P. ROAZEN, *supra* note 16, at 278–79.

96. Severo, *Mental Patients Seek 'Liberation' in Rising Challenge to Therapies*, N.Y. TIMES (December 11, 1978).

97. Allen, *Law and Psychiatry: An Approach to Rapprochement* in L. ROBERTS, S. HALLECK, AND M. LOEB, eds., COMMUNITY PSYCHIATRY (Madison: University of Wisconsin Press, 1966) 195–98; P. SCHRAG, MIND CONTROL (New York: Pantheon Books, 1978) xvi; Wald, *supra* note 79, at 993.

98. It was estimated in the late 1970s that some 7 million Americans were undergoing traditional forms of therapy and that 10 million more had recently completed such treatment. M. GROSS, THE PSYCHOLOGICAL SOCIETY (New York: Random House, 1978) 318.

99. The competition for funds and public esteem between established therapies like psychiatry and clinical psychology and other programs claiming therapeutic efficacy is discussed in Eliot, *It's All in the Mind*, NEW REPUBLIC 17–19 (August 5 and 12, 1978).

100. An important discussion of various aspects of these problems is N. KITTRIE, THE RIGHT TO BE DIFFERENT (Baltimore: Johns Hopkins University Press, 1971).

101. J. DELGAD, PHYSICAL CONTROL OF THE MIND: TOWARD A PSYCHO-CIVILIZED SOCIETY (New York: Harper and Row, 1969).

102. F. PERLS, GESTALT THERAPY VERBATIM (New York: Bantam Books, 1970) quoted in M. GROSS, *supra* note 98, at 294.

103. See, *e.g.*, D. BELL, *supra* note 82, at 25; C. LASCH, *supra* note 76, at xviii.

104. ON HUMAN NATURE (Cambridge: Harvard University Press, 1978) 185. And see W. PERCY, THE MESSAGE IN THE BOTTLE (New York: Farrar, Straus, and Giroux, 1976) 54–55: "I do not refer only to the special relation of layman to theorist. I refer to the general situation in which sovereignty is surrendered to a class of privileged knowers, whether these be theorists or artists."

105. "The trouble with the consciousness movement is not that it addresses trivial or unreal issues but that it provides self-defeating solutions." C. LASCH, *supra* note 76, at 104. See also *id.* at 51, 99; D. BELL, *supra* note 82, at 13–14; W. PERCY, *supra* note 104, at 55–56.

106. *Supra* note 82, passim.

107. "All binding engagements to communal purpose may be considered in the wisdom of the therapeutic doctrine, too extreme." *Id.* at 242. See also D. BELL, *supra* note 82, at 5–6, 72, 244–45.

108. London, *The Morals of Psychotherapy*, COLUMBIA UNIVERSITY FORUM 38 (Fall 1961). The problem of the ends of therapy provides one of the themes for Peter Shaffer's play, *Equus* (New York: Avon Books, 1975) 74, 124–25. See also E. FROMM, PSYCHOANALYSIS AND RELIGION (New Haven: Yale University Press, 1950) 73.

109. That the concepts of cure or improvement in psychosurgery engender sharp conflicts of values is apparent in the literature. See, *e.g.*, S. CHOROVER, FROM GENESIS TO GENOCIDE (Cambridge: M.I.T. Press, 1979) 137, 142; Edgar, *Legal and Public Policy Problems with Behavior Control Therapies* (Am. Ass. for the Advancement of Science, Sec. of Health, Behavior and Social Processes, December 25, 1972); Hodson, *Reflections Concerning Violence and the Brain*, 9 CRIM. L. BULL. 684–702 (1973); Neville, *Ethical and Philosophical Issues of Behavior Control* (Am. Ass. for the Advancement of Science, Sec. of Health, Behavior and Social Processes, December 27, 1972); P. SCHRAG, *supra* note 97, at 166. At an earlier period, similar conflicts surrounded evaluation of the "therapeutic" uses of castration. M. HALLER, EUGENICS (New Brunswick, N.J.: Rutgers University Press, 1963) 48.

110. F. ALLEN, *supra* note 3, at 103–05.

111. See, *e.g.*, Stiller and Elder, *PINS: A Concept in Need of Supervision*, 12 AM. CRIM. L. REV. 33 (1974); Sussman, *Judicial Control over Noncriminal Misbehavior*, N.Y.U. L. REV. 105 (1977).

112. Conflicts between the legal and popular concepts of self-defense are not unique to American society. There is evidence of such tension in

Russia both in the past and in the contemporary Soviet Union. V. CHALDIZE, CRIMINAL RUSSIA (P. Falla trans.) (New York: Random House, 1977) 130.

113. Zimring, *Dealing with Youth Crime: National Needs and Federal Priorities* (September 1975) (unpublished). During the same period the number of nonwhite persons aged 18–20 in urban communities increased over 350 percent.

114. M. IGNATIEFF, *supra* note 34, at 165–66.

115. "Blacks, Mexicans, Puerto Ricans and members of other racial minorities now constitute the majority of American prisoners." Jacobs, *Race Relations and Prisoner Subculture*, 1 CRIME AND JUSTICE 1 (1979).

116. "As the socio-cultural distance between the clinician and his patient increases, diagnoses become less accurate and dispositions more nonspecific." Gross, *The Effect of Race and Sex on the Variation of Diagnosis and Disposition in a Psychiatric Emergency Room*. J. NERVOUS AND MENTAL DISEASE 638 (No. 6, 1969). See also Allen, *supra* note 97, at 193–95. The impact of social distance between patient and therapist was noted in the American nineteenth century. Rothman quotes an institutional superintendent in the 1850s as follows: "As a class, we are not so successful in our treatment of them [the foreign born] as with the native population of New England. It is difficult to obtain their confidence, for they seem jealous of our motives." D. ROTHMAN, *supra* note 33, at 284. See also *id.* at 252–54; 262; A. DE TOCQUEVILLE, *supra* note 46, at 27–28.

117. W. LEWIS, *supra* note 5, at 157–59.

118. C. BROWN, WEILAND (New York: Doubleday, Anchor Books, 1799, 1973) 132.

Chapter 2

1. "The same public that is asked to support the criminal law and to condemn the criminal offense is also asked to embrace and provide financial resources for programs of correctional treatment that view offenders as the products of conditions over which they have little or no control. . . . The question arises whether the community can simultaneously entertain two views apparently based on such sharply divergent postulates or whether they can be accommodated with the degree of conviction necessary both to vitalize the criminal law as an effective body of regulative norms and also to advance programs of treatment realistically calculated to render its subjects less likely to offend the legal norms." Allen, *The Law as a Path to the World*, 77 MICH. L. REV. 157, 166 (1978).

2. Allen, *The Judicial Quest for Penal Justice: The Warren Court and the Criminal Cases*, 1975 U. ILL. L. FORUM 518, 522–24.

3. Among the more important works of this character is O. KIRCHHEIMER AND G. RUSCHE, PUNISHMENT AND SOCIAL STRUCTURE (New York: Columbia University Press, 1939), the influence of which may be detected in such later writings as M. FOUCAULT, DISCIPLINE AND PUNISH (New York: Pantheon Books, 1977) 24. For an evaluation of Kirchheimer and Rusche see Sylvester, *The Dilemma of the Correctional Idea*, 41 FED. PROB. 3 (June 1977).

4. See, *e.g.*, A. SALTER, THE CASE AGAINST PSYCHOANALYSIS (New York: Holt, 1952); Sears, *Survey of Objective Studies of Psychoanalytic Concepts* (Soc. Sci. Research Council, Bull. 51, New York, 1943). More relevant to the history summarized above are the early writings of Thomas S. Szasz. See his LAW, LIBERTY AND PSYCHIATRY (New York: Macmillan, 1963) and PSYCHIATRIC JUSTICE (New York: Macmillan, 1965).

5. The word *political*, which appears frequently in this discussion, is used in its broadest sense. Compare L. TRILLING, THE LIBERAL IMAGINATION (New York: Doubleday, 1953) 7, "It is the wide sense of the word that is nowadays forced upon us, for clearly it is no longer possible to think of politics except as the politics of culture, the organization of human life toward some end or other, toward the modification of sentiments, which is to say the quality of human life."

6. This characteristic of midcentury criminological writing can be illustrated by A. FINK, CAUSES OF CRIME: BIOLOGICAL THEORIES IN THE UNITED STATES 1800–1915 (Philadelphia: University of Pennsylvania Press, 1938). The discussion is almost devoid of political analysis despite the facts that it addresses topics that had immediate political consequences and a subject matter clearly related to social theory.

7. Menninger, 219 HARPER'S MAGAZINE 60 (August 1959).

8. F. ALLEN, THE BORDERLAND OF CRIMINAL JUSTICE (Chicago: University of Chicago Press, 1964) 36.

9. This tendency may be seen in Williams v. New York, 337 U.S. 241 (1949), discussed *supra* chap. 1, at note 17. More recently, the plurality opinion in McKeiver v. Pennsylvania, 403 U.S. 528 (1971), announcing that trial by jury is not constitutionally mandated in the juvenile court, speaks of "the idealistic prospect of an intimate, informal protective proceeding." *Id.* at 545. Although there may be cogent reasons for denying a Fourteenth Amendment requirement of jury trials in juvenile courts, one wonders whether "flexibility" should be considered the principal value when the issue being determined is whether the adolescent did or did not commit the delinquent act. See also the dissenting opinion of Mr. Chief Justice Burger in In re Winship, 397 U.S. 358, 375

(1970). And note the comment of Erving Goffman in ASYLUMS (New York: Doubleday, Anchor Books, 1961) 156, fn. 35.

10. A typical contemporary expression of this view is that in S. CHOROVER, FROM GENESIS TO GENOCIDE (Cambridge: M.I.T. Press, 1979) 139–40. Perhaps the ignorance or disregard of political considerations is also reflected in the slowness of American and other Western psychiatrists to perceive and protest the political uses of psychiatry in the Soviet Union. Szasz, *Soviet Psychiatry: Its Supporters in the West*, INQUIRY 4–5 (January 2, 1978). See Shapley, *U.S.–U.S.S.R. Exchange: Americans Split on Schizophrenia Program*, 183 SCIENCE 932 (1974).

11. F. ALLEN, THE CRIMES OF POLITICS (Cambridge: Harvard University Press, 1974) 30–34. And see S. SCHAFER, THE POLITICAL CRIMINAL (New York: The Free Press, 1974).

12. F. ALLEN, *supra* note 11, at 7–8. And see K. ERIKSON, WAYWARD PURITANS (New York: John Wiley, 1966).

13. F. ALLEN, *supra* note 11, at 16–17.

14. The best known of these works is D. ROTHMAN, THE DISCOVERY OF THE ASYLUM (Boston: Little, Brown, 1971). An important contributor to these views is W. LEWIS, FROM NEWGATE TO DANNEMORA (Ithaca, N.Y.: Cornell University Press, 1965). See also B. BAILYN, THE IDEOLOGICAL ORIGINS OF THE AMERICAN REVOLUTION (Cambridge: Harvard University Press, 1976) 318; D. DAVIS, HOMICIDE IN AMERICAN FICTION 1798–1860 (Ithaca, N.Y.: Cornell University Press, 1957) 121; and compare M. IGNATIEFF, A JUST MEASURE OF PAIN (New York: Pantheon Books, 1978).

15. Striking instances of this modern tendency are collected in Locke, *The Literary View: In the Cage*, N.Y. TIMES BOOK REV. (March 26, 1978) 3. See also P. SCHRAG, MIND CONTROL (New York: Pantheon Books, 1978) 235: "For a growing number of people, and to some extent for all Americans, everyday life on the outside becomes a little more like life on the inside."

16. LITTLE DORRIT (New York: Penguin Books, 1857, 1967). "*Little Dorrit* paints this entire system as a vast jail imprisoning every member of society, from the glittering admirers of Mr. Merdle to the rack-rented dwellers in Bleeding Heart Yard." E. JOHNSON, CHARLES DICKENS: HIS TRAGEDY AND TRIUMPH (New York: Viking Press, 1977) 385.

17. (New York: Viking Press, 1962).

18. E. ZAMIATIN, WE (G. Zilboorg trans.) (New York: E. P. Dutton, 1924, 1952) 167: "The latest discovery of our State science is that there is a center for fancy—a miserable little nervous knot in the lower region of the frontal lobe of the brain. A triple treatment of this knot with X-rays

will cure you of fancy."; A. HUXLEY, BRAVE NEW WORLD (London: Chatto and Windus, 1932); G. ORWELL, 1984 (New York: Harcourt, Brace, 1949).

19. "Capital punishment for economic crimes against social wealth—the forfeiting of life for an offense against social property—is an index of the importance placed on social wealth, as well as an indication that social good is more important than individual good, even if it means the exchange of life for property." R. DE GEORGE, SOVIET ETHICS AND MORALITY (Ann Arbor: University of Michigan Press, 1969) 92. In 1922 the Criminal Code of RSFSR enacted the death penalty for bribery with aggravating circumstances. "The penalty for large-scale theft or embezzlement consists of eight to fifteen years' imprisonment with confiscation of property, or—in especially grave cases—death with confiscation of property." V. CHALIDZE, CRIMINAL RUSSIA (P. S. Falla trans.) (New York: Random House, 1977) 147, 194.

20. The position has been documented in F. GRAHAM, THE SELF-INFLICTED WOUND (New York: Macmillan, 1970).

21. "The term 'social control' was first used by Clifford S. Griffin, 'Religious Benevolence as Social Control, 1815–1860' *Mississippi Valley Historical Review*, XLIV (Dec. 1957) 423–44." Banner, *Religious Benevolence as Social Control: A Critique of an Interpretation*, 60 J. AM. HIST. 23, fn. 1 (1973). Although the following works vary significantly in methods and purposes, they may be viewed collectively as expressing a social control emphasis: S. CHOROVER, *supra* note 10; M. FOUCAULT, *supra* note 14; M. IGNATIEFF, *supra* note 14; R. QUINNEY, CRITIQUE OF LEGAL ORDER (Boston: Little, Brown, 1973) and CLASS, STATE, AND CRIME (New York: McKay, 1977); D. ROTHMAN, *supra* note 14; A. SCULL, DECARCERATION: COMMUNITY TREATMENT AND THE DEVIANT: A RADICAL VIEW (Englewood Cliffs, N.J.: Prentice-Hall, 1977). A recent comment by Professor Rothman should be noted: "I am not persuaded by Foucault's assertion, nor by its corollary that crime is essentially a form of political action. . . . I would not despair, as it appears that Foucault does, of the prospects for genuine amelioration of the prison system short of a reordering of society. Change can be significant without being total." *Society and Its Prisoners: A Review of Foucault, Discipline and Punish*, N.Y. TIMES BOOK REV. (February 19, 1978) 1.

22. Quoted in AMNESTY INTERNATIONAL, POLITICAL IMPRISONMENT IN THE PEOPLE'S REPUBLIC OF CHINA (London, 1978). *Cf.* Platt and Takagi, *Intellectuals for Law and Order: A Critique of the New Realists*, 8 CRIME AND SOC. JUS. 1, 2 (Fall–Winter 1977).

23. See, *e.g., op. cit, supra* note 3, at 24, 255, 272, 277, 283. Compare the comment of Freud quoted in P. ROAZEN, FREUD: POLITICAL AND SOCIAL

THOUGHT (New York: Vintage Books, 1968) 196: "The state has forbidden to the individual the practice of wrong-doing, not because it desires to abolish it, but because it desires to monopolize it."

24. *Cf.* A. SCULL, *supra* note 21, at 11.

25. "The not-surprising devotion of these men to Protestant morality, their attachment to the capitalist economy, and their fear of democracy comprised only one strand in a complex of attitudes toward politics and society. To abstract this one strand as their 'real' motivation is to fall into the error which plagues the Progressive historians: the belief that reality is always mean, hidden, sordid and that men normally act not out of generosity but from fear and from considerations of status and gain." Banner, *supra* note 21, at 24. See also *id.* at 31; M. GRUNHUT, PENAL REFORM (Oxford: Oxford University Press, 1948) 70; M. IGNATIEFF, *supra* note 14, at 164; Talbott, *Review*, CHRONICLES OF HIGHER EDUCATION 7R (January 8, 1978); Sylvester, *supra* note 3, at 6; A. DE TOCQUEVILLE, JOURNEY TO AMERICA (J. P. Mayer, ed.) (New Haven: Yale University Press, 1959) 150. Note also the reference of Sir Karl Popper to "a widespread and dangerous fashion of our times, . . . the fashion of not taking arguments seriously, and at their face value, at least tentatively, but of seeing in them nothing but a way in which deeper irrational motives express themselves." 2 THE OPEN SOCIETY AND ITS ENEMIES (London: Routledge and Kegan Paul, 1945) 238.

26. Berlin, *Does Political Theory Still Exist?* in PHILOSOPHY, POLITICS AND SOCIETY (2d ser., P. Laslett and W. Runciman eds.) (Oxford: Blackwell, 1962) 22.

27. "The view we hold about why people commit crimes deeply influences our ways of dealing with them. There is a close relation between criminology in the strict sense of the word and penal policy." L. RADZINOWICZ, IDEOLOGY AND CRIME (London: Heinemann Educational Books, 1966) 53–54. Similar points have been made in a variety of contexts. Alper, Beckwith, and Miller, *Sociobiology Is a Political Issue* in THE SOCIOBIOLOGY DEBATE (A. Caplan ed.) (New York: Harper and Row, 1978) 481, 485–86; S. CHOROVER, *supra* note 10, at 4; P. ROAZEN, *supra* note 23, at 3; F. WOODS, MENTAL AND MORAL HEREDITY IN ROYALTY (New York: Holt, 1906) vi.

28. One aspect of this history is discussed in F. ALLEN, *Garofalo's Criminology and Some Modern Problems, op. cit. supra* note 8, at 63. And see A. FINK, *supra* note 6; PIONEERS IN CRIMINOLOGY (H. Mannheim ed.) (Chicago: Quadrangle Books, 1960); S. SCHAFER, THEORIES IN CRIMINOLOGY (New York: Random House, 1969).

29. On the nature–nurture controversy see H. CRAVENS, THE TRIUMPH OF EVOLUTION: AMERICAN SCIENTISTS AND THE HEREDITY–ENVIRONMENT CONTROVERSY (Philadelphia: University of Pennsylvania Press, 1978);

M. CURTI, HUMAN NATURE IN AMERICAN THOUGHT (Madison: University of Wisconsin Press, 1980) 272–312; N. PASTORE, THE NATURE–NURTURE CONTROVERSY (New York: King's Crown Press, 1949). And see A. Caplan ed., *supra* note 27; E. WILSON, SOCIOBIOLOGY: THE NEW SYNTHESIS (Cambridge: Harvard University Press, 1975) and ON HUMAN NATURE (Cambridge: Harvard University Press, 1978).

30. "The inherited cause of crime, or what is called 'inherent depravity' for want of a thoroughly critical analysis, produces results that seriously imperil society." *Sixty-Third Report of the Board of Inspectors of the Eastern State Penitentiary of Pennsylvania* (1893) 104; H. M. BOIES: PRISONERS AND PAUPERS (New York: Putnam, 1893); S. CHOROVER, *supra* note 10, at 145–46. See also materials cited *supra* note 28.

31. Extended discussion of the movement may be found in M. HALLER, EUGENICS (New Brunswick, N.J.: Rutgers University Press, 1963); K. LUDMERER, GENETICS AND AMERICAN SOCIETY (Baltimore: Johns Hopkins University Press, 1972).

32. M. HALLER, *supra* note 31, at 41, 67, 111–12.

33. Thus William McDougall wrote: "A nation which allows itself to drift into ultra-democracy does a grave injury to civilization, to all the higher interests of mankind." ETHICS AND SOME MODERN WORLD PROBLEMS (New York: Putnam, 1924) 192. See also Galton, *Hereditary Improvement*, 7 FRASER'S MAGAZINE 123 (1873); M. HALLER, *supra* note 31, at 6, 94, 161–62; N. PASTORE, *supra* note 29, at 27.

34. M. HALLER, *supra* note 31, at 11, 150, 159. It appears that the eugenicists were influential in inducing Congress to enact restrictive immigration legislation in the 1920s. *Id*. at 6–7.

35. *Doctors in Death Camps*, TIME 68 (June 25, 1979), quoting Robert Jay Lifton. And see S. CHOROVER, *supra* note 10, at 9.

36. "We know of no relevant constraints placed on social processes by human biology. There is no evidence from ethnography, archaeology, or history that would enable us to circumscribe the limits of possible human social organization. What history and ethnography do provide us with are the materials for building a theory that will itself be an instrument of social change." Sociobiology Study Group of Science for the People, *Sociobiology—Another Biological Determinism* in A. Caplan ed., *supra* note 27, at 280, 290.

37. See discussion *supra* chap. 1, at notes 59–61. And see D. MUNRO, THE CONCEPT OF MAN IN CONTEMPORARY CHINA (Ann Arbor: University of Michigan Press, 1977) 24–25. Occasionally comparably extreme views of human malleability have been expressed in the Western world. Thus John B. Watson wrote, "Give me a dozen healthy infants, well-formed, and my own specified world to bring them up in, and I'll guarantee to take any one at random and train him to become any type of specialist I

might select—doctor, lawyer, artist, merchant-chief and yes, even beggerman and thief, regardless of his talents, penchants, tendencies, abilities." See also L. WARD, APPLIED SOCIOLOGY (Boston: Ginn, 1906) 241, quoted in N. PASTORE, *supra* note 29, at 117.

38. *Cf.* N. CHOMSKY, REFLECTIONS ON LANGUAGE (New York: Pantheon Books, 1975) 132; D. MUNRO, *supra* note 37, at 53, 56, 89–90.

39. IN CHANCERY (New York: Scribner's, 1920, 1969) 233.

40. Quoted in M. CURTI, *supra* note 29, at 105.

41. S. FREUD, CIVILIZATION AND ITS DISCONTENTS (New York: Norton, 1961) 43. "If there is some kind of inner human nucleus, if man's instinctual dispositions set limits to culture's demands, then an empirical basis exists for the individualism of the liberal tradition." P. ROAZEN, *supra* note 23, at 159. "I think we must stop to consider whether this emphasis on biology, whether correct or incorrect, is not so far from being a reactionary idea that it is actually a liberating idea. It proposes to us that culture is not all-powerful." L. TRILLING, FREUD AND THE CRISIS OF OUR CULTURE (Boston: Beacon Press, 1955) 48. See also *id.* at 53–55. And see C. LASCH, HAVEN IN A HEARTLESS WORLD (New York: Basic Books, 1977) 132; E. WILSON, ON HUMAN NATURE (Cambridge: Harvard University Press, 1978) 79–80.

42. E. GOFFMAN, *supra* note 9, at 304–05.

43. *Philosophy and Politics* in B. MAGEE, MEN OF IDEAS (New York: Viking Press, 1978) 260.

44. "The goal of imposing manipulative routines for the purpose of effecting basic changes in 'personalities' offends us." AMERICAN FRIENDS SERVICE COMMITTEE, STRUGGLE FOR JUSTICE (New York: Hill and Wang, 1971) 146. *Cf.* T. HONDERICH, PUNISHMENT: THE SUPPOSED JUSTIFICATIONS (London: Penguin Books, 1969) 106: "It might reasonably be pointed out, on the other hand, that we certainly do influence children by other than rational means. This is so, and to some extent defensible. It might also be admitted that in certain cases behavior-therapy for adults is justifiable, even against the wishes of the individuals in question. These would be cases in which there was a danger of very great harm to particular individuals and no other more tolerable way of avoiding it." On the choice of treatment goals by the patient in psychoanalysis see W. PERCY, THE MESSAGE IN THE BOTTLE (New York: Farrar, Straus, and Giroux, 1975) 278; P. ROAZEN, *supra* note 23, at 293–94.

45. Neville, *Ethical and Philosophical Issues of Behavior Control* (Am. Assn. for the Advancement of Science, December 27, 1972) 4. See also *id.* at 15; R. BURT, TAKING CARE OF OTHERS: THE ROLE OF LAW IN DOCTOR-PATIENT RELATIONS (New York: Free Press, 1979) 108–09; S. CHOROVER, *supra* note 10, at 195–96; R. DE GEORGE, *supra* note 19, at 118; Pritchard, *Human Dignity and Justice*, 82 ETHICS 299, 309 (1972); S.

SANSWEET, THE PUNISHMENT CURE (New York: Mason and Charter, 1965) 14–15.

46. Capron, *Informed Consent in Catastrophic Disease Research and Treatment*, 123 U. PA. L. REV. 340 (1974).

47. These relations are discussed with subtlety and insight in R. BURT, *supra* note 45.

48. The antebellum history in New York is well traced in W. LEWIS, *supra* note 14.

49. The following comments were included in a manuscript prepared for oral delivery by a neurologist: "Tolerance of and encouragement of free thought is probably excellent for the high IQ bracket, but not advisable for the lower one, and one is reminded of the Roman saying: 'Quod licet Jovi non licit bovi.' . . . The problem is that the ox may not recognize himself as an ox and demand Jupiter's prerogatives. . . . Let us concentrate instead on the precise identification of the violence-prone individual. Out of the so-called rioters in Detroit, only about 10 to 15 percent were actually physically assaultive or destructive; the others mostly had a carnival. We know that it is the dumb young male who is violence prone and I emphasize now the 'male' part of the sentence." See also S. CHOROVER, *supra* note 10, at x; P. SCHRAG, MIND CONTROL (New York: Pantheon Books, 1978) 175.

50. S. SCHLOSSMAN, LOVE AND THE AMERICAN DELINQUENT (Chicago: University of Chicago Press, 1977) 191–92: "In short, the sponsors of the juvenile court infantilized the adult poor while attempting to civilize them. The extent to which the poor were humanized in the process remains, at best, ambiguous."

51. Problems of discretion surfaced very early in the American experience with the rehabilitative ideal. In the 1830s Beaumont and Tocqueville noted a controversy in Pennsylvania concerning the right granted the "houses of refuge" to receive children who had neither committed a crime nor were convicted of an offense. G. DE BEAUMONT AND A. DE TOCQUEVILLE, ON THE PENITENTIARY SYSTEM IN THE UNITED STATES AND ITS APPLICATION IN FRANCE (Carbondale, Ill., Southern Illinois University Press, 1964) 139–40. At another point the authors deal with the problem of determining the period of a child's commitment in a house of correction. "This impossibility of finding a basis for the sentence, produces a completely arbitrary execution of the law." *Id*. at 156. Ultimately they conclude that the question should be resolved, not by the courts, but by the corrections officials, because of the impossibility of foreseeing "in each case, the time which may be requisite for the correction of the vices, and the reformation of the evil inclinations of a child" when the child is first committed to the institution. *Id*. at 155. Earlier the authors had noted; "At Sing Sing, and at Auburn, there are

no written regulations: the superintendents of these prisons, have only, in their government, to conform themselves to the verbal prescriptions which they receive from the inspectors, and to a few principles expressed in the law." *Id.* at 75. See also M. GRUNHUT, *supra* note 25, at 17; M. IGNATIEFF, *supra* note 14, at 77–78.

52. Examples of such literature include Bergesen, *California Prisoners: Rights without Remedies*, 25 STAN. L. REV. 1 (1973); Paulsen, *Fairness to the Juvenile Offender*, 42 MINN. L. REV. 547 (1957); Singer, *Bringing the Constitution to the Prison: Substantive Due Process and the Eighth Amendment*, 39 U. CIN. L. REV. 615 (1970). And see F. ALLEN, *supra* note 8, at 16–23, 35–41.

53. The disease model appears very early in thought about penal rehabilitationism. Thus Plato in LAWS 9, "O sir, we will say to him, the impulse that moves you to rob temples is not an ordinary human malady, nor yet a visitation from heaven, but a madness which is begotten in a man from ancient and unexpiated crimes of his race, an ever-recurring curse." On this tendency see G. HAWKINS, THE PRISON: POLICY AND PRACTICE (Chicago: University of Chicago Press, 1976) 20; Weiler, *The Reform of Punishment* in STUDIES IN SENTENCING (Ottawa: Law Reform Commission of Canada, 1974) 124. The disease model is not a necessary premise of a rehabilitative approach, however. "Thus [one] might argue that whether or not some forms of vocational education programs reduce recidivism for some offenders is a question that can be answered apart from an assumption that job skills cure the disease of unemployment." Gottfredson, *Treatment Destruction Techniques*, 16 J. RESEARCH IN CRIME AND DELIN. 39 (January 1979).

54. *Supra* note 3, at 19.

55. "By setting no limits on the definition, there are, in effect, no boundaries on the job tasks of correctional personnel." P. LERMAN, COMMUNITY TREATMENT AND SOCIAL CONTROL (Chicago: University of Chicago Press, 1975) 80. And see AMERICAN FRIENDS SERVICE COMMITTEE, *supra* note 44, at 39–40.

56. M. GRUNHUT, *supra* note 25, at 117.

57. Robert Mark, Commissioner of the Police of the Metropolis, in Mark and Scott, *The Disease of Crime: Punishment or Treatment?* (London: The Royal Society of Medicine, 1972) 13.

58. AMNESTY INTERNATIONAL, *supra* note 22, at 59.

59. The tendency of some juvenile court judges to resist the assumptions of adversary procedures and the consequences of this propensity are revealed in W. STAPLETON AND L. TEITELBAUM, IN DEFENSE OF YOUTH (New York: Russell Sage Foundation, 1967). See also Polier, *The Gault Case: Its Practical Impact on the Philosophy and Objectives of the Juvenile Court*, 1 FAM. L. Q. 417 (1967).

60. "There is an unfortunate tendency in psychiatry and correctional administration to refer to anything that is done to offenders, even obvious punitive acts, as treatment." S. HALLECK, PSYCHIATRY AND THE DILEMMAS OF CRIME (New York: Harper and Row, 1967) 239. See also P. LERMAN, *supra* note 55, at 38, 200–01.

61. *Supra* note 55, at 83.

62. Recent statements are found in *id.* at 91–92, 199, 214.

63. "It would be churlish of us to criticize Elizabeth Fry's work. . . . Her work and its outcome is a paradigm of the drama that critics and administrators of the penal system have played over and over again: the critic attacks, devising something that seems better; the administrator co-opts the critic and implements the idea in ways and for ends quite at odds with the original intention." AMERICAN FRIENDS SERVICE COMMITTEE, *supra* note 44, at 17. A similar recurring theme appears in M. IGNATIEFF, *supra* note 14, at 128, 200, 204, 248.

64. M. GRUNHUT, *supra* note 25, at 16–17, 24–25, 30.

65. *Report on the Prisons and Reformatories of the United States and Canada* (1867), quoted in D. ROTHMAN, *supra* note 14, at 240–41.

66. M. IGNATIEFF, *supra* note 14, at 120 *et seq.*

67. M. GRUNHUT, *supra* note 25, at 91–92.

68. *Id.* at 92.

69. L. FRIEDMAN, A HISTORY OF AMERICAN LAW (New York: Touchstone Books, 1973) 519.

70. The history is sketched in D. ROTHMAN, *supra* note 14; D. SCHNEIDER, THE HISTORY OF PUBLIC WELFARE IN NEW YORK STATE, 1609–1866 (Chicago: University of Chicago Press, 1938) 333, 341–42; S. SCHLOSSMAN, *supra* note 50, at 100, 104.

71. The deliberate use of euphemistic labeling is defended with striking candor by the director of a treatment program: "Although the behaviorist usually prefers to work completely without aversive techniques, even the withholding of rewards is aversive. In certain refractory cases, deliberate painful applications are an absolutely necessary part of the treatment plan to initiate positive results. . . . The concept of punishment is largely a semantic, philosophical problem . . . which may be avoided in practice by substituting new phrases such as 'aversive conditioning' or 'negative consequences.'" Parlour, *Behavioral Techniques for Sociopathic Clients*, 39 FED. PROB. 3, 4 (March 1975). For very different emphases see A. SCULL, *supra* note 21, at 51 ("reform by word-magic"); E. GOFFMAN, *supra* note 9, at 74, "This contradiction, between what the institution does and what its officials must say it does, forms the basic context for the staff's daily activities."

72. E. GOFFMAN, *supra* note 9, at 85; F. ALLEN, *supra* note 8, at 34, fn. 12.

73. Glasser, *Prisoners of Benevolence: Power versus Liberty in the Welfare State* in W. GAYLIN, I. GLASSER, S. MARCUS AND D. ROTHMAN, DOING GOOD: THE LIMITS OF BENEVOLENCE (New York: Pantheon Books, 1978) 117; C. SILBERMAN, CRIMINAL VIOENCE, CRIMINAL JUSSTICE (New York: Random House, 1978) 324.

74. Glasser *supra* note 73, at 138–39: F. ALLEN, *supra* note 8, at 34, fn. 12.

75. Glasser, *supra* note 73, at 147; E. GOFFMAN, *supra* note 9, at 380–81.

76. G. DE BEAUMONT AND A. DE TOCQUEVILLE, *supra* note 51, at 81. This skepticism did not destroy the author's mild optimism about the prospects of penal rehabilitationism. *Id.* at 54–55.

77. On the failures of solitary confinement as a rehabilitative device, see M. GRUNHUT, *supra* note 25, at 60; M. IGNATIEFF, *supra* note 14, at 117; W. LEWIS, *supra* note 14, at 67–70. On Bentham's corporal punishment machine, see M. IGNATIEFF, at 75.

78. The tendency toward the overstatement of the rehabilitative case has been frequently noted. F. ALLEN, *supra* note 8, at 56–58; D. SCHNEIDER, *supra* note 70, at 352; Jacobs and Steele, *Prisons: Instruments of Law Enforcement or Social Welfare?* 21 CRIME AND DELIN. 348, 350–51 (1975); McPike, *Criminal Diversion in the Federal System: A Congressional Examination*, 42 FED. PROB. 10, 12 (December 1978).

79. The following comment can be strongly corroborated by anyone who has been in correspondence with American prisoners in recent years: "Indeed, one has only to refer to the growing body of writing by ex-prisoners to recognize that the subjects of prison treatment are not so much skeptical as totally cynical about the matter." G. HAWKINS, THE PRISON: POLICY AND PRACTICE (Chicago: University of Chicago Press, 1976) 21.

80. Among the competing influences was the impact of democratic politics in the Jacksonian era and in the years that followed. A. DE TOCQUEVILLE, *supra* note 25, at 67; J. JACOBS, STATEVILLE: THE PENITENTIARY IN MASS SOCIETY (Chicago: University of Chicago Press, 1977) 19–20.

81. "In all of them [prisons and asylums], no matter how philanthropic and therapeutic their original intention, there will be a tendency to modify the aims in favor of the staff, for the gap between staff and inmates to widen, for communications between them to become one way only, and for a punitive regime insidiously to appear." Mark and Scott, *supra* note 57, at 30. See also E. GOFFMAN, *supra* note 9, at 92 ("the professional in charge finds that gradually his job has been changed into a species of public relations work"); P. LERMAN, *supra* note 55, at 135; D. ROTHMAN, *supra* note 14, at 246, 270. On patient management as a motive for psychosurgery, see S. CHOROVER, *supra* note 10, at 173.

82. This is not to say that institutional personnel are invariably seduced into support of administrative and custodial measures at the expense of rehabilitative measures. Yet insistence on the latter by some institutional personnel may create dissonance that ultimately serves neither custodial nor therapeutic ends. Compare J. JACOBS, *supra* note 80, passim.

83. The ambiguity and ambivalence resulting from the competition between punitive and rehabilitative purposes is exemplified in a report of prison inspectors in 1822, "No radical change can be effected until [the prisoners'] stubborn spirits are subdued, and their depraved hearts softened by mental suffering." Quoted in W. LEWIS, *supra* note 14, at 68. Other historical and contemporary instances are described in E. GOFFMAN, *supra* note 9, at 382–83; M. IGNATIEFF, *supra* note 14, at 199; Parlour, *loc. cit. supra* note 71; D. ROTHMAN, *supra* note 14, at 102–03: S. SCHLOSSMAN, *supra* note 50, at 25, 189.

84. *Cf.* P. LERMAN, *supra* note 55, at 144–45.

85. S. SANSWEET, *supra* note 45, at 150–51, 176–77; P. SCHRAG, *supra* note 15, at 205. For punitive uses of sterilization and castration see M. HALLER, *supra* note 31, at 135, 140. The punitive purposes of juvenile justice are discussed in S. SCHLOSSMAN, *supra* note 50, at 24.

86. "One sometimes has the feeling that for reformists no expenditure could be too great if it secured an insignificant incidence of criminality." T. HONDERICH, *supra* note 44, at 106–07.

87. John Howard wrote: "Some have supposed that the profit of the work in a house of correction might support the expense of the house. But however it may appear in speculation, in practice, it is always found otherwise. The difference is great between involuntary labour and that which is performed from choice." THE STATE OF THE PRISONS IN ENGLAND AND WALES (4th ed.) (London, 1792) 41. Howard's wisdom was widely disregarded in antebellum America. "Advocates of the Auburn system commonly believed that penitentiaries should not only bear the cost of their own food, clothing, medical expenses, and staff salaries, but also pay for the charges incurred in trying and convicting inmates and in transporting the felons from the point of sentence to prison. Any profits remaining after these demands had been met could be used to maintain institutions for juvenile delinquents." W. LEWIS, *supra* note 14, at 99–100. The profit motive was strongly expressed in other movements, such as that leading to the county poorhouse system. D. SCHNEIDER, *supra* note 70, at 242. Rehabilitative gains from institutional work programs as historically practiced have been strongly doubted. E. GOFFMAN, *supra* note 9, at 10–11; M. GRUNHUT, *supra* note 25, at 217; G. HAWKINS, *supra* note 79, at 120–21.

88. AMNESTY INTERNATIONAL, *supra* note 22, at 73–75.

89. W. LEWIS, *supra* note 14, at 181–82. And see *id*. at 100–01. For a short comment on prison labor in the South, see L. FRIEDMAN, *supra* note 69, at 523.

90. L. FRIEDMAN, *supra* note 69, 522–23; M. GRUNHUT, *supra* note 25, at 228. The nineteenth-century history of prison labor in France appears to have been somewhat similar to the American experience. M. FOUCAULT, *supra* note 3, at 240–41.

91. G. DE BEAUMONT AND A. DE TOCQUEVILLE, *supra* note 51, at 119; W. LEWIS, *supra* note 14, at 109, 178.

92. Examples are discussed in A. SCULL, *supra* note 21, at 139–40, 151.

93. Similarly, whether cases are treated as problems of welfare or criminality may be determined by such considerations. An example is discussed in F. ALLEN, *supra* note 8, at 5–7. See also A. SCULL, *supra* note 21, at 54.

94. The fiscal motivations underlying many modern diversion and decarceration programs are scathingly criticized in A. SCULL, *supra* note 21. See also R. BURT, *supra* note 45, at 22–24. Modern practices may in some instances resemble the wholesale uses of probation and parole in the last century to relieve institutional overcrowdings. L. FRIEDMAN, *supra* note 69, at 522.

95. G. HAWKINS, *supra* note 79, at 49–50.

96. *What Works? Questions and Answers about Prison Reform*, PUB. INTEREST 24, 25 (Spring 1974). The article derived from a larger work. D. LIPTON, R. MARTINSON, AND J. WILKS, THE EFFECTIVENESS OF CORRECTIONAL TREATMENT (New York, Praeger, 1975). In his later work Professor Martinson has substantially modified the conclusions stated above. See Martinson, *New Findings, New Views: A Note of Caution Regarding Sentencing Reform*, 7 HOFSTRA L. REV. 243 (1979).

97. See, *e.g.*, E. GOFFMAN, *supra* note 9, at 71 ("In fact this claim of change is seldom realized, and, even when permanent alternations occur, changes are not of the kind intended by the staff."); Rittner and Platt, *The Meaning of Punishment*, 2 ISSUES IN CRIMIN. 79, 99 (1966) ("So far we have no conclusive evidence that any existing psychologically oriented treatment program achieves the objectives to which they aspire."); Ward, *Evaluation of Correctional Treatment: Some Implications of Negative Findings*, Proceedings of the First National Symposium on Law Enforcement Science and Technology (Washington, D.C.: Thompson Book, 1967); Lerman, *Evaluating Institutions for Delinquents*, 13 SOC. WORK 55 (1968); Robinson and Smith, *The Effectiveness of Correctional Programs*, 17 CRIME AND DELIN. 67 (1971). And see AMERICAN FRIENDS SERVICE COMMITTEE, *supra* note 44, at 146, "We must conclude, after decades of experimentation, that treatment has failed miserably." *Cf*. D. GLASER, THE EFFECTIVENESS OF A PRISON AND PAROLE SYSTEM (Indianapolis: Bobbs Merrill, 1964).

98. "Many correctional officials who have viewed themselves as reformers are changing their philosophies. . . . This change in the criminal justice administrators' attitude has made it difficult—sometimes impossible —to obtain support for rehabilitative projects." Halleck and Witte, *Is Rehabilitation Dead?*, 23 CRIME AND DELIN. 372, 373 (1977). *Cf.* AMERICE CAN FRIENDS SERVICE COMMITTEE, *supra* note 44, at 42. Gaylin and Rothman, *Introduction* in A. VON HIRSCH, DOING JUSTICE (New York: Hill and Wang, 1976) xxxviii.

99. See, *e.g.* Halleck and Witte, *supra* note 98, at 374–75; Palmer, *Martinson Revisited*, 12 J. RESEARCH IN CRIME AND DELIN. 133 (1975). *Cf.* Martinson, *California Research at the Crossroads*, 22 CRIME AND DELIN. 180 (1976).

100. Gottfredson, *supra* note 53. And see D. MUNRO, *supra* note 37, at 82: "A leading psychiatrist isolated what he has come to realize is a key to the failure of many attempts at reform: 'We do not really believe, most of us, that they can be rehabilitated, that they *can* change for the better, or that it is worthwhile making the effort. Would a self-fulfilling prophesy of malleability make some difference in the matter of penology?" *Cf.* Eisenberg, The "Human" Nature of Human Nature in A. Caplan, ed., *supra* note 27, at 166.

101. McCollum, *What Works!*, 41 FED. PROB. 32 (June 1977); Palmer, *supra* note 99, at 143; H. SACKS AND C. LOGAN, DOES PAROLE MAKE A DIFFERENCE? (West Hartford: University of Connecticut Press, 1979) 67.

Chapter 3

1. See discussion *supra* chap. 1, at notes 28–31.

2. F. ALLEN, THE CRIMES OF POLITICS (Cambridge: Harvard University Press, 1974) 33–35.

3. These attitudes also often express racial fears and xenophobia. Just as demands for repressive law enforcement in prior generations typically identified immigrant groups as the source of crime and disorder, similar demands today locate the primary perils in the behavior of racial and ethnic minorities.

4. On outlawry in the ancient law, see F. POLLACK AND F. MAITLAND, 2 THE HISTORY OF ENGLISH LAW (Washington, D.C.: Lawyers' Literary Club, 1959) 449: "He who breaks the law has gone to war with the community; the community goes to war with him. It is the right and duty of every man to pursue him, to ravage his land, to burn his house, to hunt him down like a wild beast and slay him; for a wild beast he is; not merely is he a 'friendless man,' he is a wolf."

5. "But both past and present experience clearly indicates that the only result to be expected from the implementation of a more punitive policy in prisons would be greatly intensified unrest, turbulence, riot and revolt, and a substantial increase in death and injury for both staff and prisoners. Because for many people, costs of that order would be regarded as prohibitive, such a strategy is quite unfeasible." G. HAWKINS, THE PRISON: POLICY AND PRACTICE (Chicago: University of Chicago Press, 1976) 46.

6. Gaylin and Rothman, *Introduction* in A. VON HIRSCH, DOING JUSTICE (New York: Hill and Wang, 1976) xxxiii.

7. A leading discussion of the impact and implications of the prisoners' rights movement is J. JACOBS, STATESVILLE: THE PENITENTIARY IN MASS SOCIETY (Chicago: University of Chicago Press, 1977) 105 *et seq.* See also Else and Stephenson, *Vicarious Expiation: A Theory of Prison and Social Reform*, 20 CRIME AND DELIN. 359 (1974); G. HAWKINS, *supra* note 5, at 140–50; Note, *Judicial Intervention in Corrections: The California Experience—An Empirical Study*, 20 UCLA L. REV. 452 (1973).

8. One may expect to see sharply increased programs of prison building in the future, however. It has been estimated that some 1,000 new prison facilities will be completed in the United States during the first half of the 1980s. Willson, *More and More Prisons*, 43 THE PROGRESSIVE 14 (December 1979).

9. "But it is surely a perverse denial of experience and totally irresponsible to abjure attempts to deal with present problems because of the prospect of an imagined futurity." G. HAWKINS, *supra* note 5, at 44.

10. It should be noted, however, that the influence of radical criminology is on the side of current inquiries into the nature and control of white-collar crime and other economic offenses. Platt, *Prospects for a Radical Criminology in the United States*, 5 CRIME AND SOCIAL JUSTICE 2 (Fall–Winter 1974).

11. See discussion *supra* chap. 1, at notes 59–69.

12. *Cf.* Wilson, *Crime and Criminologists*, 58 COMMENTARY 47 (July 1974).

13. On the inappositeness of substantive criminal law reform as an occasion for achieving significant social and political changes, see Allen, *Offenses against Property*, 339 THE ANNALS 57, 76 (January 1962).

14. "The genuinely retributive penologist believes that the enforcement of atonement is a proper aim of penal systems whether or not this enforcement reduces the incidence of the offenses in question, and whether or not it protects the offender against official retaliation." Walker, *The Aims of Punishment*, Evidence before the Royal Commission on the Prison System 1–13 (1967) in F. ZIMRING AND R. FRASE, THE CRIMINAL JUSTICE SYSTEM (Boston: Little, Brown, 1979) 698. An interesting modern at-

tempt to state a just deserts theory is that in A. von Hirsch, *supra* note 6, at 69 *et seq*. "For the principle, we have argued, is a requirement of justice, whereas deterrence, incapacitation, and rehabilitation are essentially strategies for controlling crime." *Id*. at 75. A strongly contrasting deterrent view may be found in E. van den Haag, Punishing Criminals (New York: Basic Books, 1975) 25, "From the punishment actually dispensed no benefit need be expected beyond the benefit inherent in doing what had been threatened."

15. T. Sellin and M. Wolfgang, The Measurement of Delinquency (New York: John Wiley, 1964). See also A. von Hirsch, *supra* note 6, at 78, 82, 90.

16. Among the important statements of the retributive position are those of Immanuel Kant, "In every punishment, as such, there must first be justice, and this constitutes the essence of the notion." Critique of Practical Reason, sec. 8, theorem 4. "Juridicial punishment can never be administered merely as a means of promoting another good either with regard to the criminal himself or to civil society, but must in all cases be imposed only because the individual on whom it was inflicted *has committed a crime*." The Science of Right 2. 49, E. See also Aquinas, Summa Theologica 1–2. Q 87, A 2; Hegel, The Philosophy of Right 1. 99. On the positions of Voltaire and Beccaria, see M. Maestro, Voltaire and Beccaria as Reformers of Criminal Law (New York: Columbia University Press, 1942).

17. F. Allen, *supra* note 2, at 34–35.

18. For brief discussion see M. Maestro, Cesare Beccaria and the Origins of Penal Reform (Philadelphia: Temple University Press, 1973) 20 *et seq*.

19. The difficulties of definition inherent in the concept of just deserts, however, do not necessarily invalidate its use for the purposes of penal policy. "To grant that there are difficult or even undecidable cases goes no way to committing one to the conclusion that all or even many cases are undecidable or even particularly difficult." T. Honderich, Punishment: The Supposed Justifications (London: Penguin Books, 1969) 40.

20. F. Allen, Law, Intellect, and Education (Ann Arbor: University of Michigan Press, 1979) 115–17.

21. A striking instance of reliance on the mens rea doctrine by the courts of a totalitarian regime in a case of political criminality may be found in International Commission of Jurists, Justice Enslaved (The Hague, 1955) Document No. 7, at 14. See also *id*. at 78, 81.

22. A striking illustration is John Rawls's A Theory of Justice (Cambridge: Harvard University Press, Belknap Press, 1971) and the literature it has engendered.

23. P. KURKLAND, POLITICS, THE CONSTITUTION, AND THE WARREN COURT (Chicago: University of Chicago Press, 1970) 98 *et seq.*

24. Plato rejects a purely retributive justification for punishment, "Not that he is punished because he did wrong, for that which is done can never be undone, but in order that in future times, he, and those who see him corrected, may utterly hate injustice, or at any rate abate much of their evil doing." LAWS 11. 934. See also PROTAGORAS 324; GORGIAS 525. A similar view is expressed by Hobbes, "We are forbidden to inflict punishment with any other design than for correction of the offender, or direction of others." LEVIATHAN 1. 15; see also *id.* 2. 30. *Cf. supra* note 16.

25. Allen, *The Law as a Path to the World*, 77 MICH. L. REV. 157, 161–63 (1978).

26. F. ALLEN, *Criminal Law and the Modern Consciousness*, *supra* note 20, at 93 *et seq.*

27. The uncertainties of this process have been frequently noted. Thus Hegel wrote: "Reason cannot determine, nor can the concept provide any principle whose application could decide whether justice requires for an offense (i) a corporal punishment of forty lashes or thirty-nine, or (ii) a fine of five dollars or four dollars ninety three, four &c., cents, or (iii) imprisonment of a year or three hundred and sixty-four, three&c., days or a year and one, two, or three days. . . . Reason itself requires us to recognize that contingency, contradiction, and show have a sphere and a right of their own, restricted though it be, and it is irrational to strive to resolve and rectify contradictions within that sphere. Here the only interest is that something be actually done, that the matter be settled and decided somehow, no matter how (within a certain limit.)" THE PHILOSOPHY OF RIGHT (T. Knox trans.) 3. 214.

28. "No. The Mikado's aim of letting the punishment fit the crime belongs to Gilbert and Sullivan, not to the real world of criminal justice nor to a jurisprudence of imprisonment." Morris, *Punishment, Desert, and Rehabilitation* in F. ZIMRING AND R. FRASE, *supra* note 14, at 745.

29. "It is clear that no penalty can be regarded as either equivalent or not equivalent in any factual sense, to man's culpability for his offense. This is so because the distress of a penalty and the culpability of an offender are not commensurable. There are not common units of measurement." T. HONDERICH, *supra* note 19, at 28. See also Bittner and Platt, *The Meaning of Punishment*, 2 ISSUES IN CRIMIN. 79, 81 (1966); Walker, *loc. cit. supra* note 14.

30. *Supra* note 15.

31. *Loc. cit. supra* note 28.

32. In the language of Jeremy Bentham the principle is that of "frugality": "Punishment, it is still to be remembered, is in itself an experience; it is in itself an evil. Accordingly that fifth rule of proportion is, not to produce

more of it than what is demanded by the other rules." An Introduction
to the Principles of Morals and Legislation (J. Burns and H. L. A.
Hart eds.) (London: Athlone Press, 1970) 179. See also N. Morris, The
Future of Imprisonment (Chicago: University of Chicago Press, 1974)
60–62.

33. Struggle for Justice (New York: Hill and Wang, 1971) 144.

34. Disparities in sentencing provide one of the most frequently discussed
     themes in modern correctional literature. In addition to the materials al-
     ready cited, see Diamond and Zeisel, *Sentencing Councils: A Study of
     Sentencing Disparity and Its Reduction*, 43 U. Chi. L. Rev. 109 (1976); Fair
     and Certain Punishment (Report of the Twentieth-Century Task
     Force on Criminal Sentencing) (New York: McGraw-Hill, 1976); D.
     Fogel, We Are the Living Proof (Cincinnati: W. H. Anderson, 1975);
     Partridge and Eldridge, *The Second Circuit Sentencing Study: A Report to the
     Judges of the Second Circuit* (Federal Judicial Center, 1974); Zeisel and Dia-
     mond, *Search for Sentencing Equity: Sentence Review in Massachusetts and
     Connecticut*, 1 A.B.F. Res. J. 883 (1977). Compare Martinson, *New Find-
     ings, New Views: A Note of Caution Regarding Sentencing Reform*, 7 Hofstra
     L. Rev. 243 (1979): "A favorite method of past reformers of our
     sentencing statutes might be called the 'indignant method.' . . . This 'in-
     dignant method' is not only unscientific, it is, by definition, sporadic."

35. Thus it is said in A. von Hirsch, *supra* note 6, at 93, "For sentencers'
     judgments of offenders' deserts will perforce be rather crude: e.g., such
     judgments will have to be made mainly by reference to the typical case,
     overlooking significant differences among individual transgressions."
     Of course, there must be some limits imposed on the process of awarding
     mitigations of punishment on the basis of circumstances peculiar to the
     person or his particular case. "The law," says Ernest van den Haag, "in
     attempting to mete out equal punishment, cannot and does not assume
     equal temptation." *Supra* note 14, at 99. Indeed, mitigations of punish-
     ment predicated on the peculiarities of the particular case, if carried to
     extremes, are subversive to the idea of responsibility. Criminal responsi-
     bility is predicated on the notion that individuals may generally be ex-
     pected to resist criminal inducements in situations of stress, situations not
     afflicting the majority of persons at any particular time. Yet given the
     limitations of judicial fact-finding and the inevitable imprecision of leg-
     islative definitions of crime, dangers of such subversion are not real in
     the actual administration of criminal justice, and a wider area exists for
     concern about the commensurability of penalties to culpability than some
     modern sentencing proposals allow.

36. F. Frankfurter, *The Zeitgeist and the Judiciary* in Law and Politics (A.
     Macleish and E. Prichard, Jr. eds.) (New York: Harcourt, Brace, 1939) 6.

37. A very similar actual case is reported and discussed in J. Andenaes,
     Punishment and Deterrence (Ann Arbor: University of Michigan Press,
     1974) 78–79.

38. Walker, *supra* note 14, at 699–700.

39. Goldstein, *Police Discretion Not to Invoke the Criminal Process: Low-Visibility Decisions in the Administration of Justice*, 69 YALE L. J. 543 (1960); N. MORRIS AND G. HAWKINS, THE HONEST POLITICIAN'S GUIDE TO CRIME CONTROL (Chicago: University of Chicago Press, 1970) 91.

40. One of the most effective statements of these points is in Zimring, *A Consumers Guide to Sentencing Reform: Making the Punishment Fit the Crime*, HASTINGS CENTER REP. (December 1976). See also R. CARLSON, THE DILEMMAS OF CORRECTIONS (Lexington, Mass.: Lexington Books, 1976) 91; C. SILBERMAN, CRIMINAL VIOLENCE, CRIMINAL JUSTICE (New York: Random House, 1978) 292; Tonry, *The Sentencing Commission in Sentencing Reform*, 7 HOFSTRA L. REV. 315, 324 (1979), "Reform proposals can be considered sensibly only in terms of how they accommodate, or can be manipulated by, discretion they do not abolish or structure."

41. A substantial literature on sentencing reform appeared in the 1970s. In addition to materials already cited, special mention should be made of the *Symposium on Sentencing* published in the first two issues of volume 7, HOFSTRA LAW REVIEW. Another useful and impressive study is Coffee, *Repressed Issues of Sentencing Accountability, Predictability, and Equality in the Era of the Sentencing Commission*, 66 GEO. L. J. 975 (1978).

42. See, for example, H. L. A. HART, PUNISHMENT AND RESPONSIBILITY (New York: Oxford University Press, 1968), 75 *et seq*.

43. An important modern discussion of the problem of predictability is that in N. MORRIS, *supra* note 32, at 62–73.

44. *Cf.* R. CARLSON, *supra* note 40, at 121: "None of these developments can be patched together to make a whole, much less a whole greater than the sum of the parts. They are not derived from some corpus of theory about how to treat the crime problem. Each has its own sponsorship, its own constituency. There is no theoretical glue to hold them together."

45. H. SACKS AND C. LOGAN, DOES PAROLE MAKE A DIFFERENCE? (West Hartford: University of Connecticut Law School Press, 1979) 80: "Evidence for this is the fact that the proportion of crimes committed that eventually result in arrest, conviction, and imprisonment—and therefore in parole—is very low. Thus, concentration on recidivism, rather than general prevention, may be inefficient from a utilitarian standpoint." And see A. Reiss, Jr., *Understanding Changes in Crime Rates* in INDICATORS OF CRIME AND CRIMINAL JUSTICE: QUANTITATIVE STUDIES (S. Feinberg and A. Reiss, Jr. eds.) (Washington, D.C.: Law Enforcement Assistance Admn., 1979).

46. E. VAN DEN HAAG, *supra* note 14, at 59.

47. J. JACOBS, *supra* note 7, at 206; see also *id*. at 119, 179.

48. "The irony . . . is that the rehabilitative ideal—which was supposed to redefine the inmate's status—resulted in more violence, worse general living conditions, and fewer pragmatic opportunities. The food was

worse. There was more fear, more violence, and more sexual assault." *Id.*
at 85–86. The influence or dominance of inmates in the governance of
prisons, of course, has not been limited to rehabilitative regimes. Such
influence has also been exercised in autocratic custodial regimes. The
consequences for order and security are often different, however, because although prison administration in the latter regimes may be powerless to prevent inmate influence, it is often able to determine who
among the inmates will be possessed of power and to impose limits on inmate activity in the interests of institutional security.

49. That the prisons produce physical and moral deterioration in their inmates has been asserted from the earliest days of penal reform. J.
HOWARD, THE STATE OF THE PRISONS IN ENGLAND AND WALES (4th ed.)
(London, 1792) 8–10. The proposition has been repeated in the last decade. Thus the late Hans Mattick wrote, "It is not unfair to say that if
men had deliberately set themselves the task of designing an institution
that would systematically maladjust men, they would have invented the
large, walled, maximum security prison." Quoted in G. HAWKINS, *supra*
note 5, at 45. See also Halleck and Witte, *Is Rehabilitation Dead?* 23 CRIME
AND DELIN. 372, 380 (1977); Robinson and Smith, *The Effectiveness of
Correctional Programs*, 17 CRIME AND DELIN. 67, 71–72 (1971); Sarri, *The
Rehabilitative Failure*, 7 TRIAL 18 (1971); S. WEBB AND B. WEBB, ENGLISH
PRISONS UNDER LOCAL GOVERNMENT (London: Longmans, Green, 1922)
247–48. For the view that the effects of the prison experience on the inmates is temporary and weak, see Irwin and Cressy, *Thieves, Convicts and
the Inmate Culture*, 10 SOC. PROB. 142 (1962). See also G. HAWKINS, at 63 *et
seq.*

50. A. R. M. CROSS, PUNISHMENT, PRISON AND THE PUBLIC (London: Stevens
and Sons, 1971) 36.

51. R. CARLSON, *supra* note 40, at 34–35, 99–100.

52. "It should have been no surprise, therefore, to find that in surveying the
writings of the critics of the prison system we found no absolute aboli-
tionists and that, even in the case of those unequivocally committed to
the abolition of prisons, this goal was seen as contingent on some very
substantial changes being made in the social and economic structure of
society at some prior point in time." G. HAWKINS, *supra* note 5, at 39. And
see A. VON HIRSCH, *supra* note 6, at 111–12.

53. Bazelon, *The Hidden Politics of American Criminology*, 42 FED. PROB. 3, 8–9
(June 1978); G. HAWKINS, *supra* note 5, at 54–55 ("How rarely even the
modest objective of providing humane and decent material conditions of
life has been achieved.)."

54. That humanitarian and rehabilitative motivations are often indistinguishable is demonstrated at the very beginnings of prison reform by
such activists as John Howard. *Supra* note 49, at 465. See also Halleck

and Witte, *supra* note 49, at 379 ("Is it possible to create a benign prison environment without trying to rehabilitate offenders?).

55. J. JACOBS, *supra* note 7, at 95–100.

56. The fear is sometimes expressed that the abandonment of rehabilitative objectives in penal institutions will result in capable persons losing interest in correctional careers. Thus in Halleck and Witte, *supra* note 49, at 379, "What kind of person would want to work in an institution devoted primarily to benign warehousing?" At various times in the past the unavailability of appropriate staff personnel has limited rehabilitative efforts. M. IGNATIEFF, A JUST MEASURE OF PAIN (New York: Pantheon Books, 1978) 103–04.

57. F. ALLEN, *supra* note 2, at 38–39. The tendency of American public attitudes toward crime and corrections was the subject of complaint in the nineteenth century. In 1859 a penal reformer referred to "the wicked indifference of the masses of our people to the whole subject of crime." W. LEWIS, FROM NEWGATE TO DANNEMORA (Ithaca, N.Y.: Cornell University Press, 1965) 257.

58. G. DE BEAUMONT AND A. DE TOCQUEVILLE, ON THE PENITENTIARY SYSTEM IN THE UNITED STATES AND ITS APPLICATION IN FRANCE (Carbondale, Ill., Southern Illinois University Press, 1964) 90: "We must remark here, that the zeal of religious instructors, which is often insufficient to effect radical reform, has yet a great influence."

59. The conservatism of judicial response is reflected in Adams v. Pate, 445 F. 2d 105 (7th Cir. 1971). The case is discussed in J. JACOBS, *supra* note 7, at 108–09. See also Bergensen, *California Prisoners: Rights without Remedies*, 25 STAN. L. REV. 1 (1973).

60. E. LEMERT, SOCIAL PATHOLOGY (New York: McGraw-Hill, 1951) 68; A. VON HIRSCH, *supra* note 6, at 12–13. Compare Gaylin and Rothman, *Introduction, id.* at xxxix, "We also recognize that, while rehabilitation may have been used as an excuse for heaping punishment on punishment, it also was a limiting factor and justification for what few comforts were introduced into the lives of prisoners."

61. This note was struck at the beginning of the 1970s in AMERICAN FRIENDS SERVICE COMMITTEE, *supra* note 33, at 26–27, 99: "Nonetheless, it should be clear that in the humanization of criminal justice and the provision of social services for the needy (including many convicts) we are dealing with two very different state functions. . . . [In certain European systems] opportunities for treatment are provided by agencies that have no power or effect upon the form or duration of the prisoner's term and can, therefore, serve his interests with undivided loyalty. . . . The range of voluntary services that can be made available either to defendants or prisoners is endless." The most thoughtful and persuasive statement of these matters is that of Norval Morris, *supra* note 32, at 1–57. See also Burtch

and Ericson, *The Control of Treatment: Issues in the Use of Prison Clinical Services*, 29 Toronto L. J. 51, 73 (1979); McCollum, *What Works!*, 41 Fed. Prob. 32 (June 1977); A. von Hirsch, *supra* note 6, at 115–16, 129–30.

62. *Supra* note 32, at 27.

63. The propensity of prisoners to feign rehabilitation was observed early in the history of the penitentiary. G. de Beaumont and A. de Tocqueville, *supra* note 58, at 89: "The criminal, therefore, has an interest in showing to the chaplain, with whom alone he has moral communications, profound repentance for his crime, and a lively desire to return to virtue. If these sentiments are not sincere, he nevertheless will profess them." See also American Friends Services Committee, *supra* note 33, at 97–98; P. Lerman, Community Treatment and Social Control (Chicago: University of Chicago Press, 1975) 11.

64. Beaumont and Tocqueville, writing in 1832, observed, "Experience shows that the criminal who, while in society, has committed the most expert audacious crimes, is often the least refractory in prison." *Supra* note 58, at 67.

65. Whether or in what cases voluntary participation of the subject in a therapeutic effort is indispensable to its success, may still be said to be imperfectly understood. The importance of voluntarism to success has been strongly asserted: "It may be said in general that the effectiveness of the psychotherapies is proportional to the degree of cooperation that is present." Council of the American Psychiatric Association, *Position Statement on the Question of Adequacy of Treatment*, 123 Am. J. Psych. 1458, 1459 (1967). See also R. Burt, Taking Care of Strangers: The Rule of Law in Doctor-Patient Relations (New York: The Free Press, 1979) 39; S. Sansweet, The Punishment Cure (New York: Mason and Charter, 1975) 11–12.

66. *Cf.* E. van den Haag, *supra* note 14, at 190.

67. Michael Ignatieff's critique of nineteenth-century English penal reform is relevant here: "The reformers did extend the state's obligation to prisoners, but not on the basis of a full recognition of their rights as human beings. Their right to decent treatment remained conditional on their willingness to reenter the moral consensus." *Supra* note 56, at 214. See also McCollum, *supra* note 61.

68. Jacobs and Steele, *Prisons: Instruments of Law Enforcement or Social Welfare?* 21 Crime and Delin. 341, 348, 352 (1975); W. Lewis, *supra* note 57, at 82; H. Sacks and C. Logan, *supra* note 45, at 88.

Epilogue

1. Halleck and Witte, *Is Rehabilitation Dead?* 23 Crime and Delin. 372, 382 (1977).

2. Gottfredson, *Treatment Destruction Techniques*, 16 J. RESEARCH CRIME AND DELIN. 39 (January 1979).

3. Halleck and Witte, *supra* note 1, at 377. *Cf.* R. CARLSON, THE DILEMMAS OF CORRECTIONS (Lexington, Mass.: Lexington Books, 1976) 96; E. VAN DEN HAAG, PUNISHING CRIMINALS (New York: Basic Books, 1975) 189.

4. THE LIBERAL IMAGINATION (New York: Doubleday, Anchor Books, 1953) 214.

5. R. DE GEORGE, SOVIET ETHICS AND MORALITY (Ann Arbor: University of Michigan Press, 1969) 3, 101.

6. "When we neglect the weak and helpless, the disenfranchised and disadvantaged, we betray our loving nature and endanger the social future that depends on our caring." Gaylin, *In the Beginning: Helpless and Dependent* in W. GAYLIN, I. GLASSER, S. MARCUS AND D. ROTHMAN, DOING GOOD: THE LIMITS OF BENEVOLENCE (New York: Pantheon Books, 1978) 34–35.

Index

American Friends Service Committee: attack on rehabilitationism, 7; quoted, 72, 109n44, 112n63
Aquinas, Thomas, 4, 92n11
Aristophanes, 4
Aristotle, 4
Augustine, 4

Banner, Lois W., 106n21, 107n25
Beaumont, Gustave de: reports on antebellum prisons, 12; quoted, 51, 123n58, 124n64
Beccaria, 67
Bentham, Jeremy: mentioned, 52; quoted, 119–120n32
Berlin, Isaiah, 40
Black, Justice Hugo, 5
Blameworthiness. *See* Just deserts theories
Brown, Charles Brockden, 31, 96n56

Capital punishment: in the United States, 8; in China, 18; present vogue of, 63
Carlson, Rick J., 121n44
Chalidze, Valery, 106n19
China, People's Republic of: views of education, 16–17, 22; and rehabilitation, 16–18; reliance on confessions, 17, 48, 98–99n64; penal practices, 17–18; fiscal motivations in prisons, 55; theories of malleability, 64–65
Coke, Sir Edward, 49
Confessions: importance in China, 17, 48; importance in juvenile courts, 48
Crime: public attitudes toward, 8, 35, 93–94n27

Crime causation: social factors in, 3, 14; biological factors in, 3, 41–43; theories of, 6–7, 40–44; demographic factors, 30
Criminal justice: not principally rehabilitative, 56; limits on equality of, 75; primacy of deterrence in, 77
Criminal procedure: enlargement of personal rights in, 33; rehabilitation and adversary justice, 47–48; Chinese, 48; capriciousness of early modern, 67; egalitarianism and modern law of, 68
Criminal responsibility: and rehabilitationism, 3; full autonomy as a policy assumption, 78; and mitigation of punishment, 120n35
Criminology: twentieth-century theories, 6–7; new orthodoxy in, 57–58; modern controversies, 58; research inadequacy, 58; classic theories, 67; need for research funding, 86. *See also* Radical criminology
Cross, Rupert, 80

Davis, David, 91n5
Debasement of rehabilitation. *See* Rehabilitative ideal
Decarceration: fiscal motivations, 56, requires rehabilitative technique, 80
Decriminalization: as evidence of value consensus, 29
De George, Richard T., 97n61, 106n19
Delgado, Jose M. R., 26
Dependency: exploited by modern psychologism, 26–27; in modern society, 89

127

Politics *(continued)*
    lative function, 71; rehabilitative
    programs and public anxiety, 79;
    defined, 104*n*5
Pollock, Sir Frederick, 116*n*4
Popper, Sir Karl, 107*n*25
Prisoners: cynicism about rehabilita-
    tion, 52; as aliens, 62–63; rights of
    inconsistent with "war theory", 63;
    rights of versus rehabilitation, 78;
    avoidance of deterioration of,
    79–80; feigning rehabilitation, 83.
    See also Prisons
Prisons: New York's "silent system",
    13; Pennsylvania system, 13; as a
    metaphor for society, 37; motives
    of early reform, 37; loss of
    rehabilitative goals, 49–50; waning
    of reformatory movement, 50;
    system-maintenance activities in,
    53; antebellum fiscal motivations,
    55; convict labor, 55; order in
    rehabilitative regimes, 78; decency
    of and rehabilitative efforts, 80–
    82; decency of as a task for judges,
    81–82; public attitudes toward,
    82; building programs in the
    1980s, 117*n*8; dominance of in-
    mates in, 122*n*48. *See also* Prisoners
Psychiatry: burgeoning of, 25; capa-
    cities to rehabilitate, 33
Psychologism: pervasiveness, 25–26;
    and sense of dependency, 26, 27;
    and individualism, 27; and loss of
    social purpose, 27, 28. *See also*
    Therapy
Psychosurgery: results of, 29; as a
    treatment device, 45
Public policy: as a concern of law, 1;
    and cultural change, 1; nature of
    modern analyses, 61

Radical criminology: versus reha-
    bilitation, 9; and social control
    theories, 40; offers no viable

alternatives, 64; rejects just deserts
    theories, 69–70; and white-collar
    crime, 117*n*10
Radzinowicz, Leon, 107*n*27
Rehabilitative ideal: modern decline
    of, 1, 2, 7–10; dominance of, 1, 5,
    6–7; in antebellum America, 1,
    12–16; definition of, 2–3; reli-
    gious motivation, 3, 12, 40; means
    employed, 3–4, 52; biblical expres-
    sions of, 4; in the eighteenth cen-
    tury, 4; Greek expressions of, 4;
    medical analogy, 4; medieval ex-
    pressions of, 4; reflects cultural
    context, 5, 33; and the universi-
    ties, 6–7; and legislation, 7–8; at-
    tacks on, 7–10, 32–34; goals of, 11,
    12, 14–15, 28, 29, 30; requisite
    conditions for, 11–12; and
    antebellum social reform, 14;
    antebellum skepticism, 16, 32, 54;
    penal labor as a means, 17; and
    education, 22; and psychologism,
    27–28; failure of consensus on
    goals, 28, 29, 30; modern absence
    of requisites, 28, 29, 30; demo-
    graphic causes of decline, 30; and
    hostility to authority, 30; race as a
    cause of decline, 30; social dis-
    tance and decline, 30, 31; political
    criticism of, 33; absence of politi-
    cal analysis, 34–35; and theories of
    human nature, 40; and eugenics,
    42; and liberal political values,
    44–46; as a threat to procedural
    rights, 47–49; conceptual vague-
    ness, 47, 51–52; assumption of be-
    nevolent motive, 48–49; tendency
    toward compulsion, 48–49, 86–87;
    tendency toward debasement,
    49–57; prevalence of euphemisms,
    50–51, 82; versus interests of pe-
    nal institutions, 53; versus punish-
    ment and deterrence, 53–54;
    versus fiscal motivations, 54–56;